Tony Noble needs no introduction to anyone who knows Northamptonshire, and few people could be better qualified to be the author of this book. He is the author of some twenty books, including the highly-successful *Northamptonshire, A Portrait in Colour*; *Exploring Northamptonshire*; *Northampton: a town guide*; *Exploring Parish Churches in Northamptonshire* and *Waterside Walks Around Northamptonshire*.

He was born and lived for many years in Staffordshire before his career as a teacher brought him to Northamptonshire in 1973 as headteacher of Sywell Primary School. He took early retirement in 1996 having been headteacher of Moulton Primary School for fourteen years and a pioneer of Grant Maintained Education during the early 1990's.

He currently leads a busy life supporting his family with their own business ventures as well as being a committed Christian and church warden of Sywell church and maintaining and developing his garden.

NORTHAMPTONSHIRE BEDSIDE BOOK

*A Collection of Prose
and Poetry*

SELECTED AND INTRODUCED BY
TONY NOBLE

THE DOVECOTE PRESS

First published in 2002 by The Dovecote Press Ltd
Stanbridge, Wimborne, Dorset BH21 4JD

ISBN 1 904349 05 6

© Introductions, Tony Noble 2002

Typeset in Monotype Sabon
Printed and bound in Singapore

A CIP catalogue record for this book is available
from the British Library

1 3 5 7 9 8 6 4 2

CONTENTS

INTRODUCTION

What are the requirements for a book at bedtime, when you are beginning to switch off from the day's stresses and strains? The 'Bedside Book' evolved as a collection of pieces which could be dipped into, providing light, entertaining and humorous reading without exerting too many demands on the mental processes, as the day drifts into oblivion and sleep.

Northamptonshire, my adopted county of almost thirty years, offers beautiful countryside, picturesque villages, and the valleys of the Nene and Welland cutting through large areas of pastureland, with the 'spires' and the influence of the 'squires' dominating the landscape.

I have tried to cover most aspects of Northamptonshire life and tradition and include passages which 'visit' most areas of the county, thus giving variety and empathy to the reader. Inevitably I have included several well-known and, I am sure, much loved items, but I hope that many pieces will be new to the general reader. Indeed, many extracts will never have appeared in book form and provide fascinating reading. For ease of reading I have for the most part modernised the spelling and punctuation of items, leaving where necessary the original proper names.

As a retired headteacher the temptation to include a 'Chalk and Talk' section could not be resisted and begins with John Graves asking for more and concludes with Thomas Bell's experiences as a school master – experiences I know well!

As ever, I must acknowledge the help of friends and in particular Don Slater, librarian at the University of Leicester, Department of Adult Education, University Centre Library Northampton, and to my wife and family for their patience and long suffering and the 'bouncing off' of ideas over the months.

TONY NOBLE, 2002

I · THE COUNTRYSIDE

Our County

George Harrison (1876-1950) was a well-known author and artist who travelled around the county writing a series of articles for the Kettering and Wellingborough newspapers. Many of the small sketches that begin each of the chapters in this book are by George Harrison, including the one above.

Dear County of clear winding streams,
That flow through meadows cool and sweet,
Of wooded hollows, where the gleams
Of sunlight's sheen and shadows meet.
Thy sweeping uplands fold on fold
Are changeful as the breezy skies,
Where dimpled hills for ever hold
Some tender joy, some new surprise.
Here stately rivers rise to bless
The farther counties of our isle,
To give the busy towns caress
And woo the barren fields to smile.
The village homesteads nestle down

'Midst flow'ring fields and lofty trees,
Where Spring-time's hedgerow's vernal gown
Yield honeyed spoil for toiling bees.
Historic years have left their trace
On stately homes, where still remain
The scars of conflict grim and base,
The sad intrigue, the bitter pain.
Thus Barnwell's mould'ring heap of stones
(The little left of castle wall)
Speak now of passing Kings and thrones,
Of greater power above them all;
And Oundle, known through all the shires
For schools by Laxton long endowed,
A home for youths who dare aspire
To seek the culture of the proud.
Dear Naseby echoes Cromwell's name,
And Rushton breathes of Tresham's skill;
Fair Fotheringhay brings forth the sigh,
As deeds of shame for ever will.
Famed Kirby, falling to decay,
Seems like a spectre from the past,
When gallants met in bright array,
Till greed and lust brought shame at last.
Each village of thy pleasant shire
Serenely speaks of Britain's power,
In fluted aisle and pointed spire,
In regal home or ancient tower.
Green lanes lie near to busy town,
With fresh, lush grass for weary feet,
Thy sweeping furrows rich and brown
Abundant yield the golden wheat.
Thy leafy byways loved by Clare,
Which Cowper sought, and Dryden praised,
Were limned by East to seem as fair
As Alpine mountain crest displays.
Let others sing of counties where
Proud rivers flow to meet the sea,
Of Northern moorlands bleak and bare,

With ceaseless wind's wild ecstasy,
But I will sing of narrow lanes,
So near my home on every side,
The scent of clover after rains,
The uplands rolling like the tide,
Flat meadows set by water mills,
And little paths that winding go
Through flow'ring fields and lowland hills,
With half the green world spread below.
These, these still fill my heart's desire,
And give me all the joy I ask,
In themes of loveliness entire
To mould through life my every task.

The Northamptonshire Poetry and Sketches of George Harrison (1876-1950),
*John and Vera Worledge, Jema Publications, 1996, p 10, 11, first published
1921.*

The Welland Valley

It divides and subdivides itself so much that from the mighty viaduct
which strides across its valley near Harringworth the river looks like
a few small streams. And so indeed it is; and amongst them all they
hardly offer a pool where a man may bathe with any comfort.
Nevertheless, the valley is a noble one, and, for this part of the world,
quite precipitous. Most of Northamptonshire undulates in a very
casual way; here it goes up, and there it goes down, and why it does
either of these in preference to keeping flat no one can say, but here in
the Welland, there is reason shown for the conformation of the
ground. Elsewhere, it gives few reasons for its vagaries. Here it gathers
itself together and descends abruptly to the meadows through which
the Welland flows, and rises in gentler, but still notable, hills on the
other side. From all of the many villages which dot the sides of the
valley extensive views can be had, without the trouble of climbing the
church tower, and in most of them the traveller with architectural
tastes need not go to nature for his amusement.

Northamptonshire Notes and Queries, *Vol III, 1890, p 2.*

An Apple Without a Core

Thomas Fuller, born in Aldwinkle, succinctly describes the county.

The land is as fruitful and populous as any in England . . . there is little waste ground in this, as in any county in England (no mosses, mears, fells, heaths . . . where elsewhere fill so many shires with much emptiness); Northamptonshire being an apple, without a core to be cut out, or rind to be pared away.

Worthies of England, *Thomas Fuller, 1662.*

The Natural Landscape

Steane's description of the English landscape and its geological and contrasting formation gives the reader a wonderful panoramic view of the county. The description of Salcey Forest in the autumn, or as he writes, the equivalent of New England in the fall, with its fiery reds and oranges, and the twentieth century ubiquitous motorcar making the urban sprawl of town development possible are wonderful descriptions, almost of a bygone age.

Christopher Saxton, the Tudor cartographer, published the first map of the county in 1576. His survey, though mildly inaccurate in some ways, brings out the fundamental physical contrast between the hills of the high country in the west, and the Nene valley in the centre and north-east. He shows a series of pudding-like shapes which represent the uplands and these diminish when the wriggling line which marks the course of the Nene is reached.

Most of these uplands lie over 400 feet above sea level and they stretch from Daventry in a north-east direction, ending near Stamford in Lincolnshire where the river Welland has worn a valley through. The traveller along the M1 motorway is hardly conscious that he is passing across the main watershed of Midland England; perhaps all he notices is a long gradual uphill gradient to the Watford gap. This is not surprising, because the surface of these Northamptonshire uplands is rounded and undulating; the principal underlying strata are the intractable, but not unduly hard, heavy clays of the Middle and Upper Lias, often blanketed by a thick mantle of Boulder Clay. All the sharper features have been smoothed away by the long process of denudation. The landscape is predominantly green, since there is a good deal of permanent pasture, and it is not wildly exciting. The long, level views are criss-crossed by a web of hedgerows with trees, mostly ash, punctuating the field boundaries at intervals. Innumerable spinneys give the wrong impression that the country is well wooded. They are simply the vestigial scraps of a once thick and almost total forest cover. There are few considerable views to be gained because the vantage points are scarce. The highest points are Arbury Hill, about 800 feet, Charwelton Hill, over 700 feet, and Naseby, over 600 feet. These uplands do not strike the observer as a formidable barrier but from the watershed spring the sources of the Welland, Nene and Ouse whose waters flow ever more slowly and circuitously over the level fen and silt lands to the Wash. In the south the Cherwell rises near Charwelton; its willow-lined course forms the boundary of the shire in its extreme south-west corner as it goes south into Oxfordshire on its way to the Thames. The source of the Avon is found in the uplands near Naseby, on the north-west side of the hill; it trickles west and then flows south-west out into Warwickshire and eventually joins the Severn.

As one drives south of Daventry, and even more noticeably if one bicycles or walks, one is conscious of being in a much hillier region. Between Daventry and Brackley is the area which might be called 'The Wolds'. Much of the land is again above 400 feet, but here the undulations are sharper and more frequent. The light soils of the Oolite Series, the Upper and Middle Lias predominate, and there is less Boulder Clay. The smaller fields, the network of winding roads and the fact that the villages are spaced at closer intervals, all suggest that the comparatively favourable conditions for cultivation produced a denser settlement pattern already in early medieval times.

The Nene valley occupies the centre of this laurel-leaf-shaped shire and provides its most distinctive feature. Whenever you journey across the county you are never far from the Nene. The name of the river seems to be connected with Old English words meaning 'it snows' or 'it rains' or perhaps 'to be brilliant'. Another possibility is that the name means 'to wash'. The grey, rather oily and not very rapid waters of the Nene have evidently changed somewhat in nature in the last 1500 years, but the river seen on a late afternoon in high summer, bank-brimming with the reflection of full-leaved trees in its shimmering waters, can be of surpassing beauty. It has cut a broad valley through the Great Oolite Limestone, the Estuarine Series and the Northampton Sands with their underlying clays of the Lias. These rocks form low and unimpressive hills on either side but they provided ideal settlement sites along the spring lines to the Anglo-Saxons. The alluvial soils and gravel terraces have been continuously occupied and farmed since Neolithic times. The valley was for long a main channel of communication and the occasional bridging points were magnets for urban trade at Peterborough, Oundle, Wellingborough and Northampton from the early Middle Ages onwards. Only in the twentieth century has the ubiquitous motorcar made urban sprawl and, latterly, planned-town development, possible on any scale in other parts of the countryside. The higher land to the west of the Nene is dissected by a series of gentle tributary-valleys such as the Stowe Brook, the Ise, the Harper's Brook, and, past Fotheringhay, the Willow Brook. Between these are spurs of low hills jutting out eastwards.

To the east of the Nene valley, running from Whittlebury to Lutton, is a narrow belt of country which spreads into Buckinghamshire and Bedfordshire, forming a low watershed between the basins of the Nene and the Ouse. This is composed of the Great Oolite Limestone in the south and Oxford Clay in the north, masked by great depths of drift Boulder Clay left by the glaciers of the last Ice Age. It has produced a flattish, rather dull landscape. Here were great tracts of woodland in early historic times; Whittlewood and Salcey Forests on the cold clays about 400 feet above sea level, Yardley Chase and the western part of the forest of Bromswold. Some of the dotard oaks surviving in Salcey date back to Elizabeth I's reign. Salcey forest in the autumn is Northamptonshire's nearest equivalent to the New England Fall. The whole tree-scape glows with fiery reds and oranges for a few weeks in late September and October. Only in one place is there a marked physical division; this is where the river Tove cuts a winding tributary course south-eastwards to the Ouse, and here the Upper Lias Clays are exposed.

North of the Nene lies Rockingham forest. This covered an extensive area from Kettering to Stamford and between Nene and Welland in the early Middle Ages. Settlement was sparse here and agricultural development came late. The complex of Jurassic

Limestones and Cornbrash, covered on the higher ground by drift Boulder Clay, produced a heavily wooded region, famous for hunting, and later for timber. Despite the heavy exploitation by open-cast mining of the underlying Northampton ferruginous sandstone, the modern Ordnance Survey maps still record large green patches in this area, indicating a great extent of tree cover.

Farther north again and forming the county boundary with Leicestershire and Rutland between Market Harborough and Stamford is the river Welland. The valley side is more steeply scarped than the Nene, and the heights over looking it, notably at Rockingham and Gretton, provide some of the few extensive panoramic views which the county has to offer over the watermeadows of the Welland to the green patchwork of fields of Leicestershire.

The Northamptonshire Landscape, *J.M. Steane, Hodder and Stoughton, 1974,*

Summer Moods

Often regarded as the 'Peasant Poet' and later, when locked in an asylum for the last twenty seven years of his life, the 'Mad Poet', what Clare achieved was a miracle. Clare was a poet of great power, with a tremendous range of poems - nature, love songs, lyrical, ballads and sonnets were all part of his repertoire.

> I love at eventide to walk alone,
>   Down narrow lanes o'erhung with dewy thorn,
> Where from the long grass underneath, the snail
>   Jet-black creeps out and sprouts his timid horn.
> I love to muse o'er meadows newly mown,
>   Where withering grass perfumes the sultry air,
> Where bees search round with sad and weary drone
>   In vain for flowers that bloomed but newly there;
> While in the juicy corn, the hidden quail
>   Cries 'Wet my foot!' and, hid as thoughts unborn,
> The fairy-like and seldom seen land-rail
>   Utters 'Craik, craik,' like voices underground.
> Right glad to meet the evening's dewy veil,
>   And see the light fade into glooms around.

John Clare 1793-1864

Wheat Prices

The following account of wheat and other prices, mainly in Northamptonshire, was compiled early in the nineteenth century:

1438. A famine so great that bread was made from fern roots.

1464. This year wheat sold in Northampton market at twenty pence per quarter.

1540. The dry summer. Springs and wells were dried up. In the same year was the great snow, and a frost that lasted upwards of nine weeks, so that cattle were almost lost and men would give one score of sheep for keeping another.

1596. This year wheat was at five shillings and eight pence a strike (bushel), and many died for want of food.

1630. In this year wheat was sold at nine shillings a strike.

1644. The average price of wheat for the year for the whole of England was 61s. 3d., and in 1648 75s. 6d.

1649. This year wheat sold for ten shillings a strike (80s. 0d. a quarter).

1653. Wheat sold for 18d., barley 14d., rye 16d., and malt 20d. a strike. English average for the year 31s. 6d. per quarter.

1654. Average price of wheat in England for the year, 23s. 1d.

1693. Corn was at a most extravagant price this year; wheat sold at 7s. 0d. a strike, and barley 3s. 8d. English average for the year 60s. 1d. per quarter.

1743. Average price of wheat in England for the year 22s. 1d. a quarter. The average in 1744 was exactly the same. These were the lowest averages on record.

1755. Wheat sold at 3s. 3d. and malt at 2s. 9d. a bushel. The year's average for the whole country was 30s. 1d. per quarter.

1756. Food riots in various parts. Masses of people seized corn and sold it at 5s. 0d. a bushel. The year's average for the whole country was 40s. 1d. per quarter.

1757. Prices at Northampton Market, 17th September, wheat 6s. to 7s. a bushel; October 1st, old wheat 6s. 6d. to 7s., new wheat 6s. to 7s.; October 8th, wheat 5s. 8d. to 6s. 8d. per bushel. The year's average for the whole of England was 53s. 4d. There were food riots all over the country.

1766. Our Market was last Saturday (September 27th) well supplied with Wheat and other grain, which sold at the following Prices, viz., Old Wheat from 42s. to 59s. per Quar. New Wheat 46s. to 56s. Barley 26s. to 28s. Maslin 34s. to 40s. Old Beans 30s. to 31s. 6d. New Beans 21s. to 24s. Oats 14s. to 16s. - And we have the satisfaction of being informed that we may expect a still more plentiful supply, as soon as the labourers of the several Villages in this Neighbourhood, many of whom are making the best use they can of the present fine Weather, and earning good Wages abroad, shall return to their usual Occupations of Threshing, and other Husbandry Business at home. In November Lord Northampton and Lord Halifax sent £250 each for the poor of the town. It was given away in bread, weekly, and with £170 collected in the town, to buy flour, it lasted for eleven weeks. The flour was sold at 2s. 0d. per stone; the common price was 2s. 10d.

1777. Assize of Bread at Northampton set on December 27th: Threepenny Wheaten loaf to weigh 1lb. 9oz. 5 drams; standard wheaten loaf, 1lb. 13 oz. 12 dr., household loaf 2lb. 10z. 6 dr.

1801. March 14, 21 and 28, wheat sold at 21s. a bushel. The year's average for England was 119s. 6d. per quarter. Rice advertised at Northampton at 52s. per cwt., ground rice 60s. and 'fine rice flour' 70s. The Northampton market returns give 90s. to 136s. a quarter for wheat on August 15th and 88s. to 104s. on August 22nd.

1819. Northampton Assize of Bread, June 19th: Threepenny loaf, wheaten, to weigh 1lb. 40z. 13 dr.

1839. Year's average for England, 70s. 6d. per quarter. This was a higher average than at any time during the 'Hungry Forties', when the highest average for the year for the country, was 69s, 5d. in 1847.

The County Magazine, *Vol 5, 1932, p 59.*

In Praise of Northamptonshire

Mountains move minds; their towering heads reveal
Depths of sky. Forests too, whose aspect
Giddies the sight with unremitting vastness;
Lakes, coasts and seas: all these impress
Our disenchanted souls. We still

Respond to the grandeur of each prospect.

But it is that unassuming shire
Where I was born that my own spirit flies,
Homing to her parks and ancient trees,
The sandstone manor and the weathered spire,
The steady river ambling to the seas.
Wherever I may live, my exiled eyes
Will seek that landscape and those gentle skies.

Trevor Hold 1939–.

Remarkable Dust Storm

An extraordinary dust-storm was experienced in Northampton and district between five and six o'clock on Thursday afternoon (July 12th). As far as reports are at present to hand, through a wide stretch of country, running almost due West and East, a remarkable storm of wind, almost cyclonic in its intensity, swept across Northamptonshire. The path of the storm was several miles in width, and the town of Northampton was well within its southern limit.

The wind raised immense quantities of dust high in the air, causing the appearance of heavy storm clouds in the sky. These dust clouds rushed along, covering everything with dust, darkening the air, and blotting out from view objects in the immediate vicinity. In Northampton it was impossible to see across the street through the impenetrable veil of dust; and for a few minutes traffic could only be carried on in possible danger. Wayfarers rushed into houses and shops for protection from the storm.

In the country, even on wide expanses of pasture, the same phenomena were noticed, showing that the dust must have been conveyed from a considerable distance.

At Castle Ashby, where the Northampton Workhouse inmates were having their annual outing, the dust temporarily blotted out the trees and the house from view. Fields of corn were laid as flat as though they had been rolled, but within a few minutes of the storm passing, the crops assumed their ordinary appearance.

The duration of the storm was six or seven minutes. Until nine o'clock the moon's disc was surprisingly red, showing that there was still much dust in the atmosphere.

A singular sight was seen near the Paper Mills, Northampton, when the storm was at its height. A flock of seagulls was noticed passing westward. It is very rare that these birds fly so far inland, even when stormy weather is approaching.

The Northampton Mercury, *July 13th, 1900.*

The Nene Valley

I love these meadows cool and sweet,
That lie so near to broad highway,
Where drooping pollard willows meet
And shimmer in the light of day.
I love the river flowing by
Tall flags and plumy-headed reeds
The flowers that match the hue of sky,
Those pure delights misnamed as weeds.

Here through the warm September noon
I linger idly and content,
And feel the sun a pleasant boon,
Though summer days be well nigh spent
I see the leaves to russet turn,
They flutter light as fairy wings,
The hawthorn buds with crimson burn,
Where perky robin sits and sings.

Beyond the river, gently rise
Those truant paths that winding go
By lofty trees to meet the skies,
With half the green world spread below,
Strange how the changing colours blend,
Through wooded depths and leafy lea,
With melting hues that have no end,
To glimmer like the restless sea.
Grey farms and hamlets nestle down

By labyrinths of oak and fir,
By little fields of gold and brown
Light floating films of gossamer,
When clouds obscure the glowing sun,
With trailing shadows softly blue
Which pass away when scarce begun.

And seated here a tender joy
Comes to me sweet with odours blown,
Unfettered and without alloy,
By beauty born from beauty's throne,
And all I ask for still abides
In flowering meads, and vaulted dome,
Of tender blue where white cloud rides
Above the scenes I name my home.

John and Vera Worledge, The Northamptonshire Poetry and Sketches of George Harrison *(1876-1950), 1996, p 13, first published 1921.*

2 · NORTHAMPTON

Daniel Defoe's Tour Of Great Britain

Daniel Defoe (1660-1731), author of Robinson Crusoe, *worked as a journalist, poet and novelist, and published accounts of tours that he made through the country, commentating particularly on the prevailing economic, industrial and social conditions – all approximately half a century before the Industrial Revolution.*

From Daventry we cross'd the country to Northampton, the handsomest and best built town in all this part of England; but here as at Warwick, the beauty of it is owing to its own disasters, for it was so effectually and suddenly burnt down, that very few houses were left standing, and this, though the fire began in the day-time; the flame also spread itself with such fury, and run on with such terrible speed, that they tell us a townsman being at Queen's Cross upon a hill, on the south side of the town, about two miles off, saw the fire at one end of the town then newly begun, and that before he could get to the town it was burning at the remotest end, opposite to that where he first saw it; 'tis now finely rebuilt with brick and stone, and the streets made spacious and wide.

The great new church, the town-hall, the jail, and all their public buildings, are the finest in any country town in England, being all new built: But he took very little notice of Northampton, or rather had never seen it, who told us of a cathedral, a chapter-house and a cloister.

The great inn at the George, the corner of the High Street, looks more like a palace than an inn, and cost above 2000l. building; and so generous was the owner, that, as we were told, when he built it, he gave it to the poor of the town.

This is counted the centre of all the horse-markets and horse-fairs in England, there being no less than four fairs in a year: Here they buy horses of all sorts, as well for the saddle as for the coach and cart, but chiefly for the two latter.

Near this town is the ancient royal house at Holmby, which was formerly in great esteem, and by its situation is capable of being made a royal palace indeed. But the melancholy reflection of the imprisonment of King Charles the First in this house, and his being violently taken hence again by the mutinous rebels, has cast a kind of odium upon the place, so that it has been, as it were, forsaken and uninhabited. The house and estate has been lately purchased by the Duchess of Marlborough; but we do not see that the house is likely to be built or repaired, as was at first discoursed; on the contrary it goes daily to decay.

The Earl of Sunderland's house at Althorp, on the other hand, has within these few years changed its face to the other extreme, and had the late earl lived to make some new apartments, which, as we were told, were designed as two large wings to the buildings, it would have been one of the most magnificent palaces in Europe. The gardens are exquisitely fine, and add, if it be possible, to the natural beauty of the situation.

From hence we went north to Harborough . . .

Daniel Defoe, A Tour Through the Whole Island of Great Britain, ed G.D.H. Cole and D.C. Browning (Everyman 1962), Vol. ii 86, 87, first published between 1724-26.

Northampton

Dear ancient town, where through the passing years
So much to change to meet the eye appears,
The Normans built thy castle and the wall
That after Naseby were both doomed to fall,
And fire and ravage swept too soon away
Medieval buildings with their decay.

The churches in that dreadful day were spared,
As if a righteous providence had cared
To keep them for thy future years of peace,
What men would learn of love and love's increase;
And latter men lit here their torch of flames
And bore it forth to bear an honoured name;
Bradlaugh and Labouchere, their deeds remain
As sweet as leafage after April rain;
Here gracious Doddridge long had ministered,
And pious Rylands preached the holy word
That gave men visions of a purer world,
When freedom's flag could safely be unfurled.
Thus through the passing years thy upward trend
Has been to praise, and with thy praise defend
The men who gave to life the pious hand
Of healing friendship to a troubled land.
Now standing here, the wistful eye can trace
The breezy upland, and the rolling space
Of meadow lands that lie beyond the town,
The new ploughed fields and fallows ochre brown,
The sleepy Nene that flows its level way
By mill and copse and hamlets old and grey.

John and Vera Worledge, The Northamptonshire Poetry and Sketches of George Harrison *(1876-1950), 1996, p 12, first published 1921.*

England's Best Market Square

During a visit to Northampton in June 1956 to help a campaign to relocate the Northamptonshire Record Office to Delapre Abbey, John Betjeman praised the county, highlighting the cobbled market square in Northampton.

I never hear of anyone saying they are going to Northamptonshire for their holidays. Northamptonshire is far too little regarded a county. It contains some of the most attractive villages in England, places like Fotheringhay and Rockingham and Plumpton, and some of the best towns, like Oundle and Thrapston. Its churches and cottages in all the variety of brown ironstone and pale limestone are full of originality and good craftsmanship. The county town of Northampton is full of treasures, Romanesque, seventeenth-century and late-Victorian - that is to say St. Peter's and St. Sepulchre's for the first, the Assize Courts and All Saints' Church for the second, and St. Mary's, St. Matthew's and St. Lawrence's for the third. But it has what must be the best market square left in England, now that Norwich has ruined its own with the new Town Hall. The cobbled square at Northampton, with its stalls and varied seventeenth and eighteenth century houses in brick, ironstone and stucco, is a thing to see of a fine evening when the stalls are still there to hide the ground-floor shop-fronts, the motor-cars are out of the way and Cowper, Clare and Doddridge seem to be near. Northampton is lucky in having pasture in its midst, with cattle grazing in the public parks of Abington and Delapre.

Spectator, *June 29 1956, 'City and Suburban' column.*

Opening of the New Town Hall May 17th 1864

Built of Northamptonshire stone, the Town Hall is a fine example of Victorian Gothic architecture. It depicts through its facade of statues, shields and scenes, much of the town and county's history.

Upon the seventeenth of May,
Was a splendid glorious day,
The bells struck up with merry call
The opening of the New Town Hall!
Our noble Mayor he gave consent
And thus to some did say,
'Dear friends you may close up your shops
And have a holiday.
Some to the Hall, and some elsewhere,
It matters not where I say,
So as you will be good young men,
Enjoying your holiday.'
Look at our noble Hall; its built so firm and strong,
And those that go to see it, will see the skill of man,
The carving there they do display,
The modern fashion of the day;
Some groups are large; and some are small,

Thither go and see them all.
The carving there none can express
The grandeur that they do possess.
Some did not think it just the thing
To first let Cardinal Wiseman in
To see the grandeur of the Hall,
He could take the pattern of it all;
But what is done we cannot undo,
Dear friends let us bid him adieu,
If I myself could rule the sway,
I'd keep him, keep him far away.
Now for our grand procession
It was a pleasant sight,
Because the sun shone brilliantly,
It made it look more nice;
Our noble Mayor dressed in his robes,
His gold chain shines so bright,
His subjects walking close behind
With joy and great delight;
The clergy passing on before,
There's one among the rest,
You know dear friends as well as I,
I still like him the best;
But hark the merry bells recall
The Opening of the New Town Hall.
Hark at our rifle bands, how splendid they do play,
The militia came to join them, upon this holiday,
And as they slowly passed that way
It was to wish the Old Hall good-bye,
With shouts and cheers they all did cry
Good-bye, good-bye, I say good-bye;
You'll see this noble building; it is complete I say,
Our noble Mayor unlocks the door, its he that holds the sway.
They all pass in with shout and cheers,
Our Mayor is seated in his chair,
They then began with prayer and praise,
To the Almighty their voices raise
With adoration it seems to say,

Upon this new town holiday.
And now dear lords and ladies
There's a little more to see,
Our noble Mayor is going himself,
To plant a handsome tree,
Oh may it grow both strong and tall
In memory of our new Town Hall,
But if perchance it dies away
It will be like the beauty of the day.

PART II
Then there's the little villa, it was so splendid gay,
While the Mayor and Lady Mayoress sat to dine,
The bands did sweetly play,
While all the bells did louder call
As they had opened the New Town Hall.
The morning concert did display
Some of the grandeur of the day;
Ladies from afar and ladies near,
With smiling faces did appear;
The younger ladies splendid neat,
With sparkling eyes and rosy cheeks,
They looked like flowers so fresh and gay,
That blossom in the month of May.
Some thought the evening concert was the best,
Because the rooms were lighted up,
So large they were and very tall
It showed the beauty of them all.
With wreaths and flowers they did display
Upon this new town holiday.
Then comes our noble singers, what must I say for they,
I'm sure they strove to sing their best, upon this holiday,
Because our noble leader took his choir to train to sing,
So when they had their parts to take they better could join in;
With voices sweet and charming, with voices clear I say,
They made the Hall to echo and send their notes onhigh.
There's one more thing to recall,
Our Mayor he gave a noble ball,

Our Lady Mayoress looked so nice,
She did excel the rest,
By dancing with our latest Mayor
I'm sure she must be blest;
And then our Mayor he turned around
And soon another lady found,
They danced with such an air and glee,
Till almost came the break of day.
If perchance the Prince of Wales had come
And brought his little firstborn son,
With sweet Princess, his precious bride,
So stately walking by his side,
Our lords and ladies would smile and say,
We've had a glorious holiday.
Dear friends I have a few more words to say
Upon my townsman Shakespeare's youthful day,
When he his writing first begun, he was as silly as I am,
But now his earliest writings do recall,
And Shakespeare's name is all and all.
I have no more dear friends to say
About the new town holiday.
Of all the splendour it may display
There's none to beat the wedding day.

Northamptonshire Libraries Local Studies Collection, composed by S.A.

The Great Fire of Northampton 1675

The Great Fire of Northampton was one of the most disastrous events in the town's history. This account, signed EP, and likely to have been written by the Rev Edward Pierce (or Pearse), the vicar of Cottesbrooke, includes vivid descriptions of the raging fire and the suffering of the inhabitants. The writer even condemns the looting of the 'cruel thieves', seeking divine justice unless they repent and forgive.

I have retained much of the original language of the time but have altered to an 's; what was often written as an 'f'.

The Fire brake out about half an hour past Eleven, came on directly to the back part of the Horse-Market, strengthening itself with Ricks of Corn and Maltings, it spread out its Wing to the South, and lower end of that Market. The hideous Cry of Fire, Fire, came up post to Town: but when some heard it was so far off, and in meaner Dwellings, they made the lighter of it, and others hoped it might spend itself and go out, in a large Cherry-Ground, and other Orchards in the way.

All-Hallows Bells jangled their last and doleful Knell, presently after the Chimes had gone Twelve in a more pleasant Tune: And soon after the Wind which did fly swifter than Horse-men, carried the Fire near the Dern-Gate, at least half a Mile from the place where it began, and into St. Giles-Street in the East, and consumed every House therein, save one (formerly a Gate-House) whose end-Walls were higher than the Roof, and by them preserved. When some that were strong and active, saw the streams of Fire driven before an impetuous Wind, seeing that nothing was like to stand before it, they made all haste to shift for themselves, and to save their Goods. All hands and arms were full, all busie in laying out, and mislaying what they shall never see again. Some active Men did labour all they could to save some Houses; But what could be done in such a sudden Surprise, when so many Places were on Fire at once, and so many Timber Buildings were as fuel dried, and laid in for this dreadful Fire.

Some that consider not the confounding Circumstances that People were under, have been apt to cast, upon them the blame of dispair and Negligence: but they must be silent, when they believe upon the word of all I spake with, that all that's Burnt, was irresistibly gone in three Hours time; although I know that every House was not Burnt in that time, for some; few did not begin to Burn till Six a Clock at Night, but it was too strong to be with-flood, and past hope of being saved by that time. Had it been a leisurely Fire, proceeding in order of Houses and Streets, then Buckets might have quenched the Thirst of a dry and greedy Element; then one House might have been Blown up in Sacrifice, to have saved a Street: but this Fire would have scorned an Engine, nothing less than the opening of Windows in Heaven could have quenched its Rage. Houses were casually Blown up by Barrels of Powder, laid up for Sale, but the Fire kept up its Fury and its Way for all that. To talk now of Engines, and Blowing up of Houses, are but Suppositions, which could not then preserve a House any more than now Rebuild one. We may as widely say, had it Rained all that day, the Town might have been saved from Burning.

Distracted People! How busie were they in emptying out their Goods, labouring to be before-hand with the swift Destroyer, that came upon some of them, before their Fears had notice of it. The Fire was fled over the Town, but did not forget what it had to do and therefore brake over the spacious planted Grounds, seized upon the College-Lane, and finding there great quantities of Oil and Tallow, and other combustible Matter, brake upon the back-side of the Drapery in a little time. Some threw their Goods into their Cellars; there or no where; some into the Church (that had more time and leisure than the former) in which they were consumed with it; Others into the Churchyard, and were there turned to Ashes. The spacious Market-Hill was covered with all sorts of Wares and Goods, these the affrighted Owners were forced to leave one among another, when they were enclosed With a Wall of Fire, and only one little Door of Escape left them to run out at, by Dr. Danver's House, the only House that stands in all that Row, having no Neighbour dwelling to bear it company, nor out offices to serve its necessities, they being burnt, and it self hardly preserved. Some had better help, better conveniences of Orchards and Closes than others had; some more time than others, or else the Loss had been vastly greater. And although the Fire spoiled and consumed many Goods (it spared neither Cross nor Pump, nor Timber drawn into the Market-place for the Sessions House); yet what the Fire spared in that and other Places, cruel Thieves, that come in to spoil the Spoiled, were more Merciless than a merciless Fire. May the stolen Sugars, Fruit, Spices, Linnen, Clothes, Bedding, or what ever else these Men of Prey took by Fraud, be bitter, hot, cold, and uneasie to them, till they have eased their Consciences of so great a Guilt. But Divine Justice will take a Course with them in a more dreadful Day than that was, except they Repent, Restore, give Satisfaction, or be Forgiven.

Sir, I know you can understand without my telling you, that this miserable People were loth to leave their convenient and comfortable Dwellings; but more loth to lose their Wares and Goods; but they were forced to leave the one to a Fire that would have them, and at last forced to leave both House, and Shop, and Goods, to save their Lives. Give me leave to try, if I can make you sensible of their Condition, in a Dull and Misty and Cold representation of it: For a lively Image I cannot draw, because my Bosom cannot hold their Passions, nor my Pen weep out their Tears. No words can report the scenes, Fears, Dangers, Distractions, Carefulness, and amazedness of Young and Old, that doleful Day. Oh! the Roaring of Fire and Wind, what a Thunder in the Air! What Clouds of Smoke! What tearing cracks of Timber! Ancient Couples, Beams and Walls keeping close to one another, till forced to part, suffering themselves to be burnt inch by inch before they could be separated! But what were these to the more sensible. Out-crys of a People decreed to Ruine. If you will carry Wind and Flames and Burning Houses up and down to shew them, then and not before, will I undertake to relate what a distracted Multitude thought, speak, and did, who could not tell what to Think Speak or Do that might prove Successful. There were old Men and Women, Children and Infants, Women lying-in, others full of the Small-Pox (which had been much in Town) Mothers that gave Suck. What could this helpless Multitude do?

Rev Edward Pierce (or Pearse), 1675.

Busy Northampton – Early 19th Century

Northampton. We entered this town at an inauspicious hour, just before the evening races; but the attention and civility of the master of the George Inn gave us little occasion to complain. There is some gratification in knowing, that the house you may select for accommodation, gives bread and education to the poor. The George Inn was given by John Dryden, Esq., of Chesterton, for the maintenance of the blue-coat school, which he established here about the year 1710. The trustees appointed to superintend the charity, obtained an act of parliament to sell this house, and invest the money in the funds, for the benefit of that institution. The George Inn was purchased by a society of persons, who subscribed £50 each, and is now their property. A town where races are held, and on the evening before the sports begin, may justly be compared to the workmen of the Tower of Babel - the jargon of different provincial countrymen - mountebanks and showmen - hawkers, jockeys, and black-legs, dandies, and fine ladies - make up a motley group; while confusion, noise and uncomfortableness, are the only pleasure a non-admirer of such amusement can expect. Northampton consists of two principal streets, running north and south, and east and west; intersecting each other about midway, and each street nearly a mile in length. Most of the houses are built of a reddish coloured sandstone, dug from quarries in the neighbourhood. There are some brick buildings, and others of a yellowish stone. At the eastern extremity of the town, is a pleasant walk, called the New Walk, or Vigo Paradise Walk, and was made at the expense of the corporation.

At the farthest extremity is a spring of chalybeate water, enclosed with steps and walls, and near the upper end is another spring of clear water, known by the name of Thomas a Becket's Well. At the north side of the town is a tract of land, which, in the year 1778, was an open field of 894 acres; but in that year an act was obtained to enclose it; about 129 acres of this was allotted to the freemen of the town for cattle, etc, but it was provided in the act that the same may be claimed and used as a race-course for any two days, between the 20th of July and the 20th October.

A Tour of the Grand Junction Canal 1819, John Hassell, p 66, 67.

The Battle of Northampton

The Battle of Northampton in the Wars of the Roses took place on July 10th, 1460. Henry VI lead his army out of Northampton to meet his opponents in the meadows beyond the river around Delapre Abbey. It was a fatal strategy. It rained heavily, the ground turned into a bog and prevented the cannon being employed, whilst treachery soon led to the defeat of the king, who was captured. The queen and her son escaped.

The following fairly accurate account of the conflict is taken from Michael Drayton's Poly-Olbion, *a rhyming description of England containing thirty thousand lines. The original punctuation is retained which seems to have been adopted to indicate pauses in reading and to be independent of grammatical construction.*

Then fair Northampton next, thy Battle place shall take
Which of th' emperial war, the third fought Field doth make,
'Twixt Henry call'd our sixt, upon whose party came

His near and dear allies, the Dukes of Buckingham,
And Somerset, the Earl of Shrewsbury of account,
Stout Viscount Beaumount, and the young Lord Egremount,
'Gainst Edward Earl of March, son to the Duke of York,
With Warwicke, in that war, who set them all at work,
And Falkonbridge with him, not much unlike the other;
A Nevill nobly born, his puissant father's brother,
Who to the Yorkists' claim, had evermore been true,
And valiant brother Bourcher, Earl of Essex and of Eau.
The King from out the town, who drew his horse and foot,
As willingly to give full field-roomth to his force,
Doth pass the River Nen, near where it down doth run
From his first fountain's head, is near to Harsington,
Advised of a place, by Nature strongly wrought,
Doth there encamp his power; the Earl of March who sought
To prove by dint of sword, who should obtain the day,
From Towcester train'd on his powers in good array,
The vaward Warwicke led (whom no attempt could fear);
The middle March himself and Falkonbridge the rear.
Now July entered was, and ere the restless sun,
Three hours' ascent had got the dreadful fight begun
By Warwicke, who a straight from Viscount Beaumont took,
Defeating him at first, by which he quickly broke
In, on th' emperial host, which was a furious charge,
He forc'd upon the field, itself more to enlarge.
Now English bows, and bills, and battle-axes walk,
Death up and down the field in ghastly sort doth stalk.
March in the flower of youth, like Mars himself doth bear
But Warwicke as the man whom Fortune seem'd to fear,
Did for him what he would, that whereso'er he goes,
Down like a furious storm, before him all he throws;
So Shrewsbury again of Talbot's valiant strain,
(That fatal scourge of France) as stoutly doth maintain,
The party of the King; so princely Somerset,
Whom th' others' knightly deeds, more eagerly doth whet,
Bears up with them again; by Somerset opposed
At last King Henry's host being on three parts enclos'd,
And aids still coming in upon the Yorkists' side

The Summer being then at height in all her pride,
The husbandman, then hard upon his harvest was;
But yet the cocks of hay, nor swaths of new-shorn grass,
Strew'd not the meads so thick, as mangled bodies there,
So that upon the banks, and in the stream of Nen,
Ten thousand well resolv'd, stout native English men,
Left breathless, with the rest great Buckingham is slain,
And Shrewsbury whose loss those times did much complain,
Eagremont, and Beaumont, both found dead upon the field,
The miserable King, inforc'd again to yield.

Northamptonshire County Magazine, *Vol 5, 1932, p 301, 302.*

Laying the Stone

Lady Knightley of Fawsley kept extensive diaries of her activities as well as those of her husband, who was for a number of years a Member of Parliament. In this diary entry Lady Knightley and her husband Rainald attend the laying of the foundation stones of St. Matthew's church.

MONDAY 21 SEPTEMBER 1891, FAWSLEY

Rainald and I went down to Northampton to be present at the laying the first stone of St. Matthew, Kingsley Park, a new church which is to be built entirely at Mr Phipps expense as a memorial to his late father Mr Pickering Phipps, Rainald's colleague and friend, for whom he had a great regard which was his reason for wishing to be present, and I went to be with my darling and I was rewarded for it was a very interesting day. The first thing was that by mistake we were shown into the vestry where we were introduced to our new Bishop, Dr Mandell Creighton, whom to our amazement we found gorgeously arrayed in a long flowing robe of white satin with a mitre on his head. Somehow or other I don't like it. The stone was laid by the Bishop of Peterborough, who has a good clear voice and then followed a luncheon at which I sat next to him.

The speaking was decidedly above the average and I was delighted with the reception my darling met with. Young Phipps spoke very nicely, but rather touched on dangerous ground when he spoke of the dead set made by the Church at the trade to which he belongs. It is extraordinary how the temperance question does divide people. It was a very long day, 8.30 to 6.30, but I was very glad we did it.

Politics and Society, The Journals of Lady Knightley of Fawsley *1885-1913*, Ed *P. Gordon, Northampton Record Society, 1999, p 182.*

3 · ROMANS AND SAXONS

Roman Camp, Borough Hill

I went out of the way through Norton, to see a great camp, called Burrow Hill, upon the north end of a hill, covered over with fern and gorse. Here is a horse-race kept, and the whole hill-top, which, is of great extent, seems to have been fortified; but the principal work, upon the end of it, is a squarish double ditch, of about 12 acres. The inner ditch is very large, and at one corner has a spring. The vallum is but moderate-a squarish work within, upon the highest part of the camp, like a praetorium. They say this was a Danish camp, and every thing hereabouts is attributed to the Danes, because of the neighbouring Daventre, which they suppose to be built by them. The road hereabouts too being overgrown with Dane-Weed, they fancy it sprung from the blood of the Danes slain in battle, and that, if upon a certain day in the year you cut it, it bleeds.

As to the camp, I believe it to be originally Roman, but that it has been occupied by some other people, and perhaps the Danes, who had new modelled the same, and made new works to the former. Consult Mr. Morton, who has discoursed very largely about it. Much cotyledon and ros solis grow in the springs hereabouts; the stone red and sandy, and brim-full of shells. I saw a fine cornuammonis lie neglected in Norton town road - too big to bring away; and where they have fresh mended the Watling-street with this stone, 'twas an amusement for some miles to view the shells in it. Hereabouts the road is overgrown with grass and trefoil, being well nigh neglected, for badness, and the trade wholly turned another way, by Coventry, for that reason. Between the head of the Cam and the river Avon, Arbury Hill is in view, another Roman Camp, upon a very high hill, notoriously made for a guard between the two rivers.

Natural History of Northamptonshire, *J. Morton, 1712.*

Chronicle of Northamptonshire

The Anglo-Saxon Chronicles provide a graphic account of the thousand turbulent years from the time of the Roman invasion to the middle of the twelfth century. Killing, pillaging, rebuilding strongholds and developing monastic orders was all part of daily life and interesting references are made to several areas of Northamptonshire.

913. By the grace of God, Aethelflaed, lady of the Mercians, went with all the Mercians to Tamworth, and built the borough there in early summer and after, before Lammas, built that at Stafford. The year after that, the other was built at Eddisbury in early summer, and the same year, late in autumn, that at Warwick.

The force rode out after Easter, from Northampton and Leicester, broke the truce and killed many men at Hook Norton and thereabouts. Very soon after that, as the other force came home, they met a second band riding, that rode out against Luton. Then the people of those parts were aware of them, and fought against them; they put them to full flight, rescued all whom they had captured, also their horses and a great part of their weapons.

914. After that, the same year before Martinmas, king Edward went to Buckingham with his troops, stayed there for four weeks, and built the strongholds on either side of the river before he left. Eorl Thurcytel sought him there for his lord, and all the eorls and most senior men who belonged to Bedford; also many who belonged to Northampton.

In this year the Danes rode out after Easter from Hamtune (Northampton) and from Leicester and slew many men at Hockerton and thereabouts. And very soon after that the one came home, then they raised another troop which rode out against Leighton, and then were the country people ware of them and fought against them and put them to full flight and rescued all that they had taken and also a great portion of their horses and weapons.

917. Before Easter, king Edward commanded the boroughs at Towcester and Wigingamere to be occupied and built up. The same summer, between Lammas and midsummer, the force broke the peace at Northampton and Leicester, and from there north. They went to Towcester, they fought against the borough all day, thinking to break in, but the people inside fended them off until more help came. They gave up the town and went away.

Quickly afterwards, the same autumn, king Edward went with the West-Saxon army to Passenham, and stayed there while the borough at Towcester was built up with stone wall; eorl Thurferth and the holds turned to him, and all the force which belonged to Northampton northwards to the Welland sought him as lord and protector.

956. ArchbishopWulfstan passed away on December 16th and was buried in Oundle.

963. And I (king Edgar), give the town that is called Oundle with all that belongs to it, that is the Eight Hundreds, with market and toll, freely, so that no king, bishop, eorl nor shire-reeve have any authority there; nor anyone but the abbot alone, and those he appoints. I give Christ and St. Peter, at the bidding of bishop Aethelwold, the lands of Barrow, Warmington, Ashton, Kettering, Castor, Ailsworth, Walton, Werrington, Eye, Longthorpe, and a minter in Stamford. Of this land and all else that belongs to the monastery, I say that it is free concerning criminal and civil jurisdiction, in matters warranty and the judging of thieves.

1011. The king and his counsellors sent to the force and entreated peace, promised them tribute and provisions on the condition that they stop their ravaging. They had by then overrun i. East Anglia, ii. Essex, iii. Middlesex, iv. Oxfordshire, v. Cambridgeshire, vi. Hertfordshire, vii. Buckinghamshire, viii. Bedfordshire, ix. half Huntingshire, x. much of Northamptonshire, all Kent, Sussex, Hastings, Surrey, Berkshire, Hampshire and much of Wiltshire.

1065. They sent after Morkere, eorl Aelfgar's son, and chose him as eorl, and he went south with all the shires, with Nottinghamshire, Derbyshire and Lincolnshire, until he came to Northampton, and his brother Edwin came to him with the men in his eorldom; also many Welsh came with him. Eorl Harold came there to meet them, and they laid on him an errand to king Edward, and also sent messengers with him, demanding that they have Morkere as their eorl. The king granted this, sent Harold to them at Northampton on the eve of St. Simon and St. Jude's Day, and informed them of the same: they renewed king Cnut's laws there. The northern men did much harm around Northampton, while they went on their errand, in that they killed men, burnt houses and corn, and took all the cattle they could find; that was many thousands and many hundreds of men they took, and led them north with them. So that shire (Northamptonshire) and the shires near it were the worse for many winters.

1137. In this evil time, abbot Martin held his abbey for twenty years . . . he fared to Rome, and there was received by pope Eugenius . . . he regained lands that powerful men held by force; William Malduit, who held Rockingham Castle, he won Cottingham and Eastern Maudit; from Hugo of Waterville he won Irthlingborough and Stanwick, and sixty shillings a year from Aldwinkle. He made many monks, planted a vineyard, made many buildings, and changed the layout of the town to better than it was before. He was a good monk and a good man, therefore God and good men loved him.

1141. Later thereafter, the king and eorl Rannulf made a settlement at Stamford, swore oaths, fastened troths that neither would betray the other - and it availed to nothing, for the king, through bad council, later seized him in Northampton and put him in prison. As soon again, on worse council, he let him out, on the condition that he swear on relics and find hostages, that he would give up all his castle.

Various sources including, The Anglo-Saxon Chronicles, *Translated and Edited by Anne Savage, 2002.*

4 · THE GRAND UNION CANAL

Waterways have been the life blood of society. The rivers carved out by successive ice ages, giving fertile valleys for the invader to settle and develop our towns and villages. Later the Grand Union Canal enabled the county's economy to flourish, and now, both in their different role, emphasise not only their historical significance, but also the wealth of wildlife amidst unspoilt beauty, as leisure activities are encouraged.

Early Beginnings, April 1769

AN ACT FOR
Making and maintaining a Navigable Canal
from the Oxford Canal Navigation, at
Braunfton, in the County of Northampton, to
join the river Thames at or near Brentford, in
the County of Middlefex, and alfo certain
Collateral Cuts from the faid intended Canal.
WHEREAS it is practicable to make and
maintain a Canal for the Navigation of Boats,
Barges, and other Veffels, from the prefent
Oxford Canal, in the Parifh of Braunfton, in
the County of Northampton, through by, or

near the Towns of Daventry, Newport
Pagnell, Leighton Buzzard, Rickmansworth,
and Uxbridge, in the feveral Counties of
Northampton, Buckingham, Bedford,
Hertford, and Middlefex . . .

Navigating the Blisworth Tunnel

*The Grand Union Canal was opened in 1805 as The Grand Junction
Canal and John Hassell's tour of the canal soon after provides an
enchanting account through the eyes of an artist, for Hassell on his
travels painted many delightful watercolours of his observations,
scenery and places. His descriptions of places nearby and activity
along the canal are still used and read today.*

Descending the hill we come suddenly upon the seven locks which lift
the navigation from the valley to the entrance of the tunnel at Stoke
Bruerne. The scenery at the first bridge we pass over is very
interesting; the view of that village, and its church on a wooded
eminence, with the approach to it by the navigation, is singularly
beautiful, and has induced us to introduce it in the work. It was
harvest time, and the avocations of the farmer appeared on every side.
The effects on the landscape was good, and the incidents natural.

These combinations charm the spectator in a common sense, but
where a number of local beauties are joined, they give a consequence
to the landscape, and make up a good subject for the painter; the
effects of light and shadow are the peculiar care of the artist, and often
render a very humble composition of the highest interest. It is like the
graceful carriage of a female, who to a lovely person and disposition,
adds the blandishments of the Graces.

Every object that encountered our sight, as we passed to the village
appeared of the picturesque; the team retiring from the glebe had its
rustic mate and tired plough boy, with all their paraphernalia, seated
on the leading horses; the navigation attendants and their cattle were
bustling to pass a lock; the freighted boats presented a motley group
of passengers on their decks; while a number of female attendants on
the canal horses, reminded me of those hardy Cambrian lasses I have
so often seen following their laborious avocations.

Stoke Bruerne village has a great affinity in appearance to the Welsh villages, the buildings very much resemble them in their make, and brought to my recollection the happy hours I have passed in traversing those mountainous regions. The church, which is an old Gothic building, is situated on the highest part of the hill on which the village stands; and there is an extensive prospect from the extremity of the churchyard, overlooking the country and the valley we had just passed. The same view presents itself from the bridge we have annexed. At the entrance of the celebrated tunnel, a succession of moving objects occur and as it is a resting place for the navigation cattle, we anticipated finding some accommodation; our wants being moderate, we felt highly gratified by our good hostess announcing her ability to supply us with an excellent piece of corned beef. The servant being from home, I undertook the nursery department, and to the tune of the Sailor's Lullaby, rocked a sweet little babe to its peaceful slumbers, while she provided vegetables to our repast. The chubby infant reminded me of the substantial comforts of *Dulce Domum*.

The canal is carried by a level above the tops of those houses which are situated at the lower parts of the village, and appears like a trench cut through a hill, made rather wider at this place than usual. A quarter of a mile brought us to the entrance of the tunnel, which is faced with brick and stone, and assimilates in its appearance with the bridges that are thrown over the stream at the requisite places. The ground above the entrance is very rugged and picturesque from its inequalities, and is topped with wood. Several barges were now preparing to enter the excavation: the men throwing off their upper garments and lighting up their lantern, gave the helm for steerage to the women, one or two females generally attending each boat; when ready they loose the two ropes of the horses, and apply themselves to the poles, with which they sturdily shove the boats through the dark channel. On the top of the hill, just above the navigation, there is a small shed erected for the attendants and cattle that have come over from Blisworth, and are to await the arrival of their proprietor's barges passing through the tunnel from that village. The distance is about two miles and a half under ground, and is usually performed by two men with a loaded boat in two hours and a quarter, but some time less if light or unladen.

A Tour Of The Grand Junction Canal in 1819, *John Hassell, p 45, 46.*

The Iron Trunk

The Grand Union Canal leaves Northamptonshire at Cosgrove where there is a spectacular viaduct called the 'Iron Trunk', which crosses the River Ouse. Early in its build it was not without disaster.

On the morning of Friday, February 19th, 1808, the inhabitants of this town (i.e., Stony Stratford) were thrown into the greatest consternation by a report that the three large aqueduct arches under the immensely high embankment made about four years previously for carrying the line of the Grand Junction Canal across the valley about a mile and a half below Stony Stratford, had fallen in and that the River Ouse was so dammed up thereby that the town must shortly be inundated to a great depth. The fears of those who hastened to the spot were much allayed by finding that one of these arches which had been propped up underneath with timber soon after the centres were struck, was still standing, and that this one arch, owing to the river not being very high, was able to carry off the water as fast as it came down. On examination of the other two arches, it appeared that about twenty-two yards of the middle part of each had fallen in and blocked up the opening, laying the canal in complete ruin, emptying it as far as the nearest stop-gates on each side. A new aqueduct bridge was opened on January 21st, 1811. It is of cast iron and is a splendid piece of engineering skill - known by the name of 'The Iron Trunk.'
The County Magazine, *Vol 5, 1932.*

The Early Capitalists

In 1818, the annual gross revenue of the canal amounted to the sum of £170,000; it possesses 1,400 proprietors; and its shares of £100 have recently sold at from £240 to £250 each. Many of the first capitalists in the kingdom are its proprietors, and its usual routine of business is so conducted as to give satisfaction to all who are connected with it.
A Tour Of The Grand Junction Canal in 1819, *John Hassell, p vi.*

Working the Canal

We lived by the canal at Stoke Bruerne, just by the bottom lock. You could look across to the big house at Stoke Park through the trees. A family called Burns lived there; and in the very bad winter of 1895, when I was six, the canal was frozen over for sixteen weeks and none of the barges could move. The Burns family used to make coppers full of soap two or three times a day and anybody who was out of work could go and have some.

Just below the bridge they fixed the horses to the ice-breaker. There must have been more than twenty of them, they stretched, sometimes one horse, sometimes two abreast, right down past the next lock to the wooden-topped bridge below that. It was a sight, all those horses with their drivers, then the steam-boats followed behind, as close as they could get, then the horse-boats. They kept going, up and down, day and night, to keep it open till it thawed.

All the boats had to come through the Blisworth Tunnel. The fare for the tug to pull the boat through was sixpence for an empty boat and a shilling for a full one. Sometimes when there was no wind, the smoke and fumes were shocking.

The boat people didn't get much money, you know. A boat with a ton of cargo got a farthing a mile. The boat would carry thirty tons, but it doesn't work out much, does it? They carried coal, long ash poles which they took to London to be made into cotton-reels, loads of corn, beer, which Phipps sent from Northampton to Coventry, limestone, ironstone from Blisworth to Hunsbury Hill furnaces, then the pig-iron from Hunsbury Hill to Birmingham, groceries and sometimes gunpowder.

The boat people were a mixed bunch. Some were clean, some were dirty. Some were honest and some were thieves. Most of them never learnt to read or write.

Northampton Chronicle and Echo, *14th November 1979.*

Lobby

Lobscouse, originally a German dish made with fish, has been adapted by the British sailors who changed it to boiled beef and is eaten by the canal folk. It has a wonderful flavour and can be enjoyed by all. Try it.

INGREDIENTS

1 lb (450g) slices of cooked beef (silverside is ideal), 1lb (450g) onions, 6 oz (170g) carrots, 3 oz (85g) parsnips, 3 oz (85g) swede, 1 ½ lb (680g) potatoes.

METHOD

Peel and coarsely slice the onions Peel the rest of the vegetables and cut them into slices about fi inch (3-4mm) thick. Put a layer of potatoes on the bottom of a large casserole dish and place on top of this the following layers: onion, beef, mixed root vegetables, potato, mixed root vegetables, beef, onion and finally potato. Pack the layers as close as possible. Pour into the casserole sufficient beef stock to almost cover the top layer of potato. Place the lid on the casserole and leave in a preheated oven at 250°F/121°C (Gas Mark fi) for two and a half to three hours.

Lobby is easy to prepare because it is a complete meal cooked in one container.

Traditional Northamptonshire Recipes, *I. Andrews, 2000, W.D. Wharton, p 149.*

5 · A LAND OF SPIRES

May Your Sins Be Forgiven

March 20 1672. Cousin Isham of Willey came with his son and told the story of a clergyman who gave a man named Wolf thirty shillings to kill his wife. Wolf promised to kill her next day. The clergyman on the following day went to his work, and after working two or three hours went home to see what had been done to his wife. As soon as he passed the threshold he found her dead on the floor. He called in his neighbours, saying that someone had killed his wife. When they came, they said he had killed her himself. He denied it, saying he had not killed her, but he was taken and condemned. When he came to the gallows he said nothing except that he had not killed her; then, seeing the hangman putting the rope round his neck, he confessed all to the hangman - that he had promised thirty shillings to Wolf to kill his wife; he begged the hangman to say nothing about it. After he was hanged, the executioner feeling uneasy told the whole story: how the clergyman had given Wolf thirty shillings to kill his wife, which Wolf proceeded to do. When they heard this they took Wolf and put him to the question. He could not deny it, and when they saw that he was guilty they shortly afterwards hanged him - a fate he richly deserved.

The Diary of Thomas Isham of Lamport ., *translated by N. Marlow.*

Christs Message

Philip Doddridge (1702-51), was a minister and teacher who made a valuable contribution to the spiritual, educational and cultural welfare of Northampton. He is best remembered for his ability to take a biblical text (often used as a sermon) and mould the words and meaning into a hymn. Typical of this and perhaps the most well known is 'Hark The Glad Sound', the theme taken from St Luke, chapter IX, verses 18 and 19.

HARK the glad sound! the Saviour comes,
The Saviour promised long!
Let every heart prepare a throne,
And every voice a song.

He comes the prisoners to release
In Satan's bondage held;
The gates of brass before him burst,
The iron fetters yield.

He comes the broken heart to bind,
The bleeding soul to cure,
And with the treasures of his grace
Enrich the humble poor.

Our glad hosannas, Prince of peace,
Thy welcome shall proclaim,
And heaven's eternal arches ring
With thy beloved name.

Philip Doddridge 1702-51.

'O Nancy, Wilt Thou Go With Me?'

Thomas Percy became vicar of Eastern Maudit in 1753 and it is said that his poetry and ballads had a profound influence on writers, as it moved away from dull, pompous and formal verse. He met and married Anne Guthridge from Rothwell and this was his proposal poem for her, which Robert Burns thought the finest ballad in the language. Percy left Eastern Maudit in 1782 to become Bishop of Dromore, County Down, returning to Ecton in retirement.

O Nancy, wilt thou go with me,
    Nor sigh to leave the flaunting town?
Can silent glens have charms for thee,
    The lowly cot and russet gown?
No longer dressed in silken sheen,
    No longer decked with jewels rare;
Say, canst thou quit each courtly scene,
    Where thou wert fairest of the fair?

O Nancy, when thou'rt far away,
    Wilt thou not cast a wish behind?
Say, canst thou face the parching ray,
    Nor shrink before the wintry wind?
Oh, can that soft and gentle mien
    Extremes of hardship learn to bear,
Nor, sad, regret each courtly scene,
    Where thou wert fairest of the fair?

O Nancy, canst thou love so true,
    Through perils keen with me to go?
Or, when thy swain mishap shall rue,
    To share with him the pang of woe?
Say, should disease or pain befall,
    Wilt thou assume the nurse's care,
Nor, wistful, those gay scenes recall,
    Where thou wert fairest of the fair?

And when at last thy love shall die,
    Wilt thou receive his parting breath?
Wilt thou repress each struggling sigh,
    And cheer with smiles the bed of death?
And wilt thou o'er his breathless clay
    Strew flowers, and drop the tender tear?
Nor, then, regret those scenes so gay,
    Where thou wert fairest of the fair?

A Collection of Poems, *Ed. Robert Dodsley, 1758.*

Luncheon v Sermon

In the early days when the London and Birmingham Railway was still under construction, passengers travelling north from London had to transfer south of Wolverton to horse-drawn coaches and travel to Rugby before rejoining the train. An early railway guide book includes an interesting story about the Rector of Passenham, who was perhaps more interested in the things of the flesh than of the spirit!

As we descend the hill into Stony Stratford, we perceive Passenham on our left; it may be distinguished by the tower of its church. The population of this parish is 828, principally rural. The present incumbent is Loraine Smith, of sporting notoriety, about whom very many singular tales are told, which are indeed almost too extraordinary to be recorded. As a specimen, we shall only give one, which appears not very improbable, and which shows that if not a very spiritual parson, he is at any rate a very hospitable man.

One morning, on coming to church on a bitterly cold day, he found that his usually not very large congregation was limited to some seven or eight persons; and having, it would appear, no very great opinion of the benefit to be derived from a sermon under such circumstances, he addressed the parties to the purport that if they would step up to his house, they should have a good luncheon of ale and beef, which would do their bodies more good than he could do their souls on such a wet morning. The *on dit* asserts, that they took his advice, and had the benefit of his kitchen, for the loss of his sermon.

The sporting anecdotes of this gentleman would fill a volume; but as they are far more creditable to the sportsman than to the clergyman, we must withhold them; hoping, as he is now in possession of his family property, that he will enter upon the station in society, viz: that of a country gentleman, which he is so eminently qualified to adorn. A more liberal man, a kinder heart, and complete gentleman (when he pleases), does not exist among the squirearchy; but certainly nature never intended him to be a clergyman.

The London and Birmingham Railway Companion, *Arthur Freeling, 1838.*

Practical Goodness,

During the nineteenth century the Rev Sir James Stonhouse, one of the founders of Northampton General Hospital, wrote a short passage on 'Hints for doing Good' titled, 'Means of doing good bodily'. Were these the first thoughts of the National Health or Private Health system?

1. By giving to the poor bread, coals, shoes, stockings, linen, coats or gowns, which may be bought much cheaper than they can buy them.
2. By paying their house-rent, or part of it.
3. By sending them wine, herb teas, or spoon meats when sick, and sometimes proper dinners on their recovery, suitable to their weak state.
4. By paying their apothecary's bill, or part of it.
5. By giving rakes, prongs, or spades, to day labourers, or some implements of their trade to poor industrious workmen.
6. By seldom giving money, unless to those who live at a distance; and then we should be well assured that their case is truly stated, and that we cannot relieve them by any other method.
7. By subscribing to an infirmary, where we may procure that relief for some real objects of compassion, which they cannot obtain elsewhere and without which, perhaps, they must perish, or remain helpless of any cure, and burdens to society.
8. By discouraging idleness in man, woman, or child; and by contriving work for those who are unemployed.
9. By defending the poor against oppression; especially such of them as are too often most grievously oppressed by hard-hearted parish officers, who have the power over them.

The County Magazine, *Vol 6, 1933, p 121.*

Holy Cure

In the parish of Marston St Lawrence, Northamptonshire, there is a notion very prevalent that rain-water collected on Holy Thursday is of powerful efficacy in all diseases of the eye. Ascension Day of the present year was very favourable in this respect to these village oculists, and numbers of the cottagers might be seen in all directions collecting the precious drops as they fell.

Northamptonshire Notes and Queries, *1854, p 542.*

Escape for a While

In Byfield church there is a notice for those taking sanctuary there after some misdemeanour.

If you took sanctuary in the church you could not be forcibly removed for forty days, during that time you had to take an oath of abjuration before a coroner and proceed to a seaport nominated by him. After forty days you went on your way penniless clothed in sackcloth and carrying a white wooden cloth, you then proceeded to the port directed by the coroner not spending more than one night in any place and not to waiver off the Queen's/King's highway. On reaching the port, if there is no vessel for him he must, daily walk into the sea up to his waist. If in forty days there is no ship then he must go into the church and start again.

The Eccentric Vicar

First, for four or five days after my decease, and until my body grows offensive, I would not be removed out of the place or bed I shall die on, and then I would be carried and laid in the same bed, decently and privately, in the summer house now erected in the garden belonging to the dwelling house where I now inhabit in Whilton, and to be laid in the same bed there, with all the appurtenances thereto belonging, and to be wrapped in a strong double winding sheet, and in all other respects to be interred as near as may be to the description we receive in Holy Scripture of our Saviour's burial, the doors and windows to be bolted, and to be kept as near in the same manner and state they shall be at the time of my decease and I desire that the building or summer house may be planted round with evergreen plants, and fenced off with iron or oak pales and painted a dark blue colour.
Extract from the will of Rev Freeman Langton, dated September 16th 1783 and Rector of Whilton.

Epitaphs

There are many ways in which people say farewell to their loved ones, some have difficulty expressing themselves, others enjoy the opportunity for light-hearted humour, perhaps reflecting their departed's character. Sadly, the strict guidelines imposed on modern memorials do not allow for the creative flair of our predecessors.

In Barton Seagrave church is a brass dated 1616 which summarises the desolation felt by the rector, having lost his young wife Jane Floyd. The brass depicts a tiny baby in a cradle and two older children in small beds with his late wife wearing an enormous ruff and hood.

> Here she was born and bred, here was she married,
> Here did she live and die, thus was she buried.
> This brass can say no more.

Culworth churchyard, recognises a loyal African slave, brought from his homeland and who was only sixteen when he died.

Charles Bacchus, an African who died in 1782. He was beloved and lamented by the family he served, was grateful and humane, and gave hopes of proving a faithful servant and a good man.

A message from Ambrose Marriott on a headstone in Sywell churchyard, dated 8th February 1888 and, being close to the path, is there for all to see.

> Stop my friend as you pass by
> As you are now so once was I
> As I am now so you must be
> So be prepared to follow me.

and a similar one at Boughton

> Time was I stood where thou dost now,
> And view'd the dead, as thou dost me;
> Ere long thou'lt be as low as I,
> And others stand and look on thee.

A generous man, a monumental tablet to his deeds is located in the porch of St Botolphs, Stoke Albany.

Here lyeth ye body of Francis Parker who gave to ye pore of this
parish ten shillings a yeare to be paid on Lamas day every yeare.
For ever, upon this grave stone.
February 4th 1683

*An amusing little ditty in Old Corby church, remembers John Lee, but
strangely, above the inscription is depicted a skull and bones!*

Here lyeth the body of John Lee
Who departed at age about sixty three,
And though his body here confined be,
his name live to perpetuity.
And when it is time then from the dust,
shall live with ye soul with the just.

*The redundant church at Blatherwycke has a wonderful tomb to the
young poet Thomas Randolf, who died in 1635 whilst on a visit to the
village. The carved memorial is written in delightful Elizabethan
English.*

Here sleepe thirteene together in one tombe
And all these greate, yet quarrell not for roome.
The Muses and ye Graces teares did meete
And grav'd these letters on ye churlish sheete;
Who having wept, their fountains drye,
Through the Conduit of the eye,
For their freind who here does lye,
Crept into his grave and dyed,
And soe the riddle is untyed,
For which this church, proud that the Fates bequeath
Unto her ever-honour'd trust,
Soe much and that soe precious dust,
Hath Crown'd her Temples with and Ivye wreath;
Which should have Laurell been,
But yt the greived Plant to se him dead
Tooke pet and withered

And in the same churchyard an unfortunate end . . .

In memory of
Anthony Williams
who was drowned
(in Blatherwycke Lake)
June 11th 1836
Aged 29 years.
Here a poor wanderer hath found a grave
who death embraced when struggling with the wave

Over indulgence has always been a problem, here leading to an unhappy end.

Sacred to the memory of
ELIZA
The beloved wife of Richard Gardner
Clerk, Curate of this Parish,
Who died on Tuesday the 17th March 1840,
Aged 36 years
And whose mortal remains are deposited
beneath the stone in the middle aisle marked with the initials EG
Her death was instantaneous arising from fright,
occasioned by a violent attack made upon the house door by
three or four men in a state of intoxication with a view to disturb
the peaceable inmates in the dead of the night.
the loss to her bereaved husband and three infant
children is humanly speaking irreparable.

Situated in the church porch at Paulerspury is a memorial to a well-known Baptist minister, who founded the Baptist Missionary Society.

TO THE GLORY OF GOD

AND IN

MEMORY OF WM CAREY

MISSIONARY AND ORIENTALIST

WHO WAS BORN AT PAULERSBURY AUGUST 17th 1761

DIED AT SERAMPORE, INDIA

JUNE 9th 1834

As his health deteriorated Philip Doddridge left Northampton for the warmer climate of Portugal. He died in 1751 and some years later one of his former pupils celebrated his life by erecting a monument over his grave.

Philip Doddridge, DD.
Died 26th Oct 1751 Aged 50
with high respect for his
character and writings, this
monument was erected in June 1828
At the expense of Thomas
Taylor, of all his numerous
Pupils the only one then living.

... and finally found in Weedon churchyard is a tombstone of an old lady, Alice Old, who could have told a tale or two, and was described by Arthur Mee in 1946 as:

A lady who lived in the reign of six sovereigns, born under Elizabeth, dying under William and Mary. She was born on the Roman Watling Street. She would hear of Drake and Raleigh, and would hear the bells tolling for Queen Elizabeth. She may have seen the Gunpowder Plot men flying for their lives towards Ashby St. Ledgers, and perhaps some survivors from Naseby Field came limping through the village. She may have seen Charles Stuart riding captive on the way from Holdenby. She would hear the tales brought from London of the Great Plague and the Great Fire, would see the red glow in the sky when Northampton town was burned down, and would hear the village bells ringing out the good news that the Stuarts were gone.

Northamptonshire, *Arthur Mee, 1946, Hodder and Stoughton, p 348.*

6 · SQUIRES

Elizabeth I's, 'Dear and Faithful Servant.'

Anthony Jenkinson, Lord of Sywell Manor, was a remarkable seaman and adventurer in the mould of Drake and Raleigh. Elizabeth's 'Dear and Faithful Servant' was keen to obtain trading concessions from Russia and the East.

The names of such countries as I Anthony Jenkinson have travelled unto from the second of October 1546 at which time I made my first voyage out of England - until the year of Our Lord 1572 when I returned last out of Russia.

First Flanders and the Low countries then Germany over the Alps, Italy then the Piemont and into France. Also through Spain and Portugal sailed the Levant sea. Been to all the Chief Islands Rhodes, Malta, Sicily, Cypress, Candu. I have been to Greece, Morea, Achia, and where the old city of Corinth stood. Turkey, Syria, Asia Minor, Damascus, Samaria, Galilee, Philistine and Palestine. Jerusalem and all the Holy Land, Africa, Algiers, etc. I have sailed far Northward within the Mare Glaciate where we had continual day and sight of the sun ten weeks together.

Norway, Lapland, Samaystia. I have travelled through the ample realms of Russia from the North Sea (to) Lapland - even to the Mare Capsium I have been in diverse countries near the Caspian Sea and discovered all the regions about Chircasse, Camul, Shafeal, Shirvieu and others. I have travelled 40 days journey beyond the said sea towards the Oriental India and Cathaia through deserts and Wilderness through 5 kingdoms of the Tartar and all the land of Turkeman and Zagatag(y) and so to the Great City of Boghar in Bactria, not without great perils and dangers some times.

After all this in 1562 I passed again of the Caspian Sea another way and landed in Armenia at a city built by Alexander the Great and from there Travelled thro Media, Parthia, Hircania into Persia to the court of the Great Sophia Called Sha(w) Tomasso unto whom I delivered letters from the Queen majesty and remained in his court 8 months then returned home.

Finally I made two voyages more out of England to Russia, one in 1566, the other in 1571 and thus being weary and growing old, I am content to take my rest in mine own house chiefly comforting myself in that my service hath been honourably accepted and rewarded of her Majesty and the rest by whom I have been employed.

Sywell, the Parish and the People, *Don Slater, Jema Publications, 2002, p 42.*

'The best arranged country seat in the kingdom'
Althorp in 1669

Cosmo III, Grand Duke of Tuscany, before he ascended the throne, paid a visit to England, as part of a tour undertaken to escape from his wife, who had a terrible temper. With him came Count Lorenzo Magalotti, who wrote an account of the Duke's travels. The Duke visited Northampton on May 12th, 1669 on his way from Cambridge to Oxford. He stayed on the night of the 12th at the George Inn in Northampton.

The following morning His highness left Northampton for Oxford, in variable weather; the road, almost the whole of the way, was uneven; and the country, for the most part uncultivated, abounding in weeds, which surround on every side the royal villa of Holdenby, a square place, situated on the highest part of an eminence, of which you have a view on the right, as you go along the road. In this villa of Holdenby, or Homby, King Charles the First was shut up by order of the Parliament on suspicion that he had attempted, with the assistance of

Lord Murray, to fly from Newcastle in the county of Northumberland, where he was kept in strict confinement by the Scots. It was all almost destroyed by the Parliamentarians in the time of Cromwell, but was restored by King Charles the Second, and given to my Lord Arlington, and afterwards sold by him to the Duke of York.

After taking a view of Homby, we entered into a park, separated by palisades from the adjacent territory, belonging to the villa of Althorp, a seat of my Lord Robert Spencer, Earl of Sunderland, who had given his highness repeated and pressing invitations to visit him there. Before he reached the villa, his highness was received and escorted by the said earl, who was anxiously expecting his arrival.

Immediately on alighting, he went to see the apartments on the ground floor, from which he ascended to the upper rooms, and found both the one and the other richly furnished. His highness paid his compliments to my lady, the wife of the master of the house, and daughter of my Lord George Digby, Earl of Bristol, by whom the Earl had three children, one son and two daughters; and when he had spent some time in this visit, the hour of dinner arrived, which was splendid, and served in the best possible style.

At table his highness sat in the place of honour, in an armchair, he having previously desired that my lady, the wife of the earl, might be seated in a similar one; the earl also was obliged by his highness to take his place close to him, the gentlemen of his retinue sitting separately upon stools.

When dinner was over, his highness was conducted through the other apartments of the mansion, all of which were sumptuously furnished and having observed the manner in which apartment communicated with another, he went down into the garden, in which, except some ingenious divisions, parterres, and well arranged rows of trees, there is little to be seen that is rare or curious; as it is not laid out and diversified with those shady walks, canopied with verdure, which add to the pleasantness of the gardens of Italy and France, but of which the nature of usage of this country would not admit.

The villa is built at the bottom of a valley, surrounded by beautiful hills, clothed with trees. To get into the court (which is situated betwixt two large branches of the building that bound two of its sides, which correspond with each other as to their shape and style of architecture, and have betwixt them the principal part of the house which is in front) we ascended a bridge of stone, under which is to run the water, which will collect in great abundance from the springs that issue from the surrounding hills.

The whole of the edifice is regularly built, both as to its exterior and interior, and is richly ornamented with stone of a white colour, worked in the most exquisite manner, which is dug from a quarry at Weldon, fourteen miles distant. If they could take off a certain natural roughness from the stone, and give it a polish, it would not be inferior to marble.

The ascent from the ground-floor to the noble storey above, is by a spacious staircase of the wood of the walnut tree, stained, constructed with great magnificence; this staircase, dividing itself into two equal branches, leads to the grand saloon, from which is the passage into the chambers, all of them regularly disposed after the Italian manner, to which country the earl was indebted for a model of the design, and it may be said to be the best planned and best arranged country-seat in the kingdom; for though there may be many which surpass it in size none are superior to it in symmetrical elegance.

At a proper hour, after dinner, his highness departed from the villa, highly gratified with the politeness of the earl, who sent him, in his own coach-and-six, as far as Brackley, a town in the county of Northampton, formerly of considerable extent, and celebrated for the fine woollen cloths which were manufactured there; at present it is merely a collection of a few houses. His highness there changed horses for the sake of expediting his journey.

They travelled from Althorp to Brackley, through a country partly in tillage and partly in pasture; and of a similar description was the road to Oxford, although it became rather flatter.

The County Magazine, Vol 6, 1933, p 14, 15, originally translated and published in 1821.

The Diary of Thomas Isham, Begun by His Father's Command on the 1st of November 1671

Written in the seventeenth century and during the reign of Charles II, this daily diary penned by Thomas Isham, who later succeeded his father as the 3rd Baronet of Lamport in 1675, illustrates a remarkable perception by a fifteen year old boy about the social and contemporary issues of the time. Ordered by his father to write the diary in Latin and as an educational exercise, Thomas was paid a substantial reward of £6 per year. It is only possible to select a few entries, (each entry is complete for that day), but the complete diary provides fascinating reading for all interested in the period after the English Civil War.

NOVEMBER 1671

1. My father first taught me the way to draw parallel lines and to divide a straight line. Father stood sponsor to the son of John Hanbury Esq. and the name given to the child was John.

5. The annual Feast was held. Father promised to pay me six pounds a year if I kept a dairy.

6. Sir William Craven and his wife, the daughter of Gilbert Clerke Esq. of Watford, dined with us. Mr Wikes came with his hounds and challenged ours to a coursing match, but the beaters could not find a hare. On the same day a very large hog was killed.

DECEMBER 1671

2. A stranger died here while on a journey, and was buried in the churchyard.

4. We heard that a girl journeying to Leicester from London had been found dead in a ditch near Creaton.

7. Mr Hanbury's butler brought someone before father because he thought the man had robbed him of four pounds.

9. While walking in the fields we saw the cowheard Bayley stealing wood from the hedges.

11. Mr Hanbury's servant, who was suspected of having taken the butler's money, was put in prison.

12. John Chapman went to London to sell the sheep.

14. Mr Whitelaw, a Scotsman, master of Guilsborough School, came to dinner, and among other things told us that the master of Shrewsbury School had been barred out by his pupils, and while trying to enter again through the window had been shot in the arm with a bullet by one of the boys. He also told us that the daughter of Stephen Langham Esq. was to be married today to a Mr Style of Kent.

23. We heard that Mr Berriman, the rector of Beddington, is dead, and that when he was dissected a stone was found in his heart.

27. The more substantial inhabitants were asked to dinner. The

Countess of Sunderland had a baby daughter. Mr Ward came to dinner.

JANUARY 1672

18. Mr Wase came to dinner and I thanked him for the book on bees which Mr Corney had procured at my request. Dorothy, daughter of Sir Edward Nicholls, was married to Mr Snagge, a gentleman of Bedford.

23. Mr Snagge's servant came over, well drunk, and said his master had gone to Lord Montagu's.

24. An honest fellow from Clipston came and said that Mr Garrard has come to Clipston. Knight of Draughton went to Northampton and on the way back got down from his horse to relieve himself, whereupon the horse slipped from his hand and returned home, leaving its master in the gorse at Pitsford.

30. Cook went to Northampton to sell the rabbit skins and sold them for six shillings.

MARCH 1672

6. Mr Richardson visited us as usual and said that a new Sessions House is to be built at Northampton, for the erection of which Sir James Langham and Sir William Langham, together with their brother Stephen Langham Esq, have contributed £300, the Earl of Peterborough £100, Lord Montagu £100 and the Earl of Northampton £20. The town of Northampton is to give £200. Mr Eyre senior told us that the Queen is very ill.

13. Mr Greene came and told us the tale of a murder committed not far from Northampton. Sir Robert Draiton went into the fields with some other gentlemen to seek recreation in hunting. While hunting the hounds refused to leave a certain place. Sir Robert Draiton, noticing this, went to them and found the body of a man who had been killed two or three days before. His ears and nose were cut off and his body so savagely mutilated that no one could recognise him. So they went to the Northampton crier to proclaim that such a man had been found, but there was no one to recognise him. So it was ordered to be put in The Gazette.

15. Today I am fifteen years old.

APRIL 1672

3. We harnessed our ass to the roller to see how he could draw, and we believe that when the ground is made more level he will do better.

11. I went to Harlestone races; there were many horses running for the silver cup, including Lord Cullen, Lord Sherard, Sir William Haslewood and Mr Digby; Lord Sherard won the prize. Lord Cullen fell from his horse and was badly hurt. There was another gentleman who rode against someone for five shillings, and when he was near the end of the course his mount stumbled over something and fell to the ground with its rider. He whole body was bruised and he rolled over unconscious.

JUNE 1672

13. Mr Eyre returned from Northampton and told us he had heard that Holland was almost crushed by the consummate skill and energy of the King of France, and that four envoys had come to our King from the Dutch to discuss peace proposals.

19. Dr Malden came and told us of an edict of the King by which no news is to be published.

23. A Dutchman has come to England with all his family and said that his country was exposed to such dangers that for two Dutch miles around Amsterdam they had flooded the fields, and that the nobles have sent their wives and children to Flanders and Zeeland for safety. De Witt has been wounded by fellow-citizens but is still alive. Utrecht and many other towns have surrendered to the King of France.

30. After the many boastings of the Dutch about their naval victory, we are now certain that their fleet has returned home, and that part of it is so mauled that several ships are beyond repair. It has turned out quite differently from what many thought; they said the Dutch would capture many of our ships, when in fact many of their own number which set sail are still missing. This is besides the incredible number of brave men and nobles who were in the ships and persished.

JULY 1672

8. Today we went to Northampton to eat cherries and Mr Richardson came with us. But when we got to Northampton we found the cherries either over-ripe or ruined by the rain; but since we were in the garden we told the gardener to bring the best fruit, for we intended to spend the greatest part of the day there. Mother sent Lewis from the garden to fetch a man who sold glass dishes. When he had agreed with Mother over the price of several, she told him to put them carefully in a basket. But when Lewis was about to count out the money for them, the rogue said that he was giving him less than

Mother had agreed; but Mother refused to give him any more, whereupon he went home scowling.

15. We went today with Mr Maidwell to Brington to see the famous tombs of the Spencer family, and it is indeed a fine sight to see such magnificent and polished sculptures. On the way back we called for a little while at Haddon at the home of Farmer Wills.

23. Cousins Isham from Barby and Willey came with their wives, and cousin Isham of Willey said that the wife of Lord Roos had died in childbirth.

AUGUST 1672

10. Today Judges Wyndham and Atkyns called here on their way to Northampton, Lord Exeter sent us some venison.

15. Mr Morgan and Mr Clerk of Loddington came and dined with us. Robert went to Northampton market to sell horses, but failed to sell a single one.

24. Sir Charles Harbord came with his two sons from Grafton, where one of them lives. We sent Bradshaw's son into the pond, where he caught five or six fish by tickling, and after dinner Sir Charles Harbord and his sons went back to Grafton.

29. The famous races were held at Irthlingborough and Mr Washbourne won a silver cup. A man came and bought our bees, he gave us a shilling a hive.

30. Twelve Oxford men agreed to go to a certain wood with pistols and swords to kill deer. They unthinkingly spoke so loud that they were easily heard by the keepers, who were prowling round the woods with cudgels to give a sound beating to anyone they caught. Soon afterwards they caught sight of six men: three turned and ran, but the rest were easily caught by the keepers although they struggled. The keepers gave them a terrific beating before letting them go and seized their best dog, for which they gave three pounds; they sent them home with empty purses, and the men returned to great disgrace, as the would-be thieves made a public spectacle of their own capture.

SEPTEMBER 1672

9. Northampton fair was held, and everything was very cheap.

14. A new horse race is to be held at Harlestone on the Thursday after Michaelmas.

19. Father bought a black horse from Hutchison which cost nine pounds. There is a widespread rumour that the Mayor of

Northampton is planning a great entertainment, for he has taken office as the first mayor elected outside the borough. He has invited all the nobility and gentry from the district and many from the whole of England, and, wishing to ingratiate himself with the people of Northampton, he has arranged a horse race at Harlestone. The petty sessions were held at Walgrave.

25. Today we picked the walnuts. Twigden brought two ferrets, which cost six shillings. The Maidwell miller took ten rabbits. A man came from Mr Perkins of Bunny in Nottinghamshire and brought a bitch on heat.

26 Mrs Mawson returned home. The Boughton miller brought several eels and a pike. We bought two eels and a pike.

30. A fox killed many hens and Blaxley's cock. The mayor of Northampton gave a magnificent feast according to custom.

JANUARY 1673

1. John Chapman went to London. Mr Greene sent his usual presents for the New Year and so did many others. Several thieves broke into Bamford's house and stole more than twelve shillings worth of tallow. They also broke Tyler's gates, but took nothing, and no one knows who they were. Four soldiers came with drums and Father gave them five shillings. Lumley's unmarried daughter is with child. Holland went with Katherine Baxter to to Sir Edward Nicholl's house.

2. A man from Leicester mended the clock which hangs in the parlour. Lumley's daughter was married to the man who seduced her. Willes of Haddon came.

5. We heard that Chapman of Draughton, being in drink in a house at Maidwell, said that Sir William Haslewood had no one in his house but sodomites and whores. When this was told to Lady Haslewood she ordered him to be turned out of his house, and two or three of them hauled him out and, seeking their opportunity, attacked him, giving him such a beating that he is not expected to live.

7. The petty sessions were held at Kettering.

MARCH 1673

15. We planted a number of apple trees in the orchard and in the sycamore walk. I am sixteen today.

17. Some men from Brixworth cleaned our pond.

19. A Brixworth man came for Mr Richardson to ask him to bury a

boy from Northampton.

23. Brother Ferdinando said his catechism in church.

27. Mr Richardson told us that Whalley, the rector of Broughton, is to marry the Archdeacon's daughter.

28. I went coursing for hares with Lewis and Robert.

JUNE 1673

5.   Father, Mother and my sister Mary went to Lord Montagu's.

6.   Lord Exeter sent a large pike with two tench to Lord Montagu who sent them to us. Our cook drew them with charcoal in the kitchen. A woman living in Brixworth lost her boy, but eventually found him sitting under a tree near Holcot bridge.

8.   Michael Wright came here drunk and talked rashly and imprudently. We could not induce him to go, so John Chapman went to Brixworth with him at ten o'clock at night.

20. Mr Meriden visited us on his return from London. He told us that the Earl of Sunderland's groom married the daughter of a rich man, unknown to her parents, who, when they found out, put the man in prison and hanged him.

24. Boughton Fair: I went with Mother and my brothers and sisters. Mr Green returned from London.

30. A clergyman named Hall, to whom Lord Montagu had given a living, showed his gratitude by calling him a scoundrel and a rogue. Lord Montagu brought an action against him and he was fined a thousand pounds. He could not pay so he decided to kill himself.

JULY 1673

8.   Today Father and I set off for Oxford with my brother Justinian. There was nothing of note on the journey except a hill near Daventry which 'overlooks valleys and houses and distant fields'. Here they say Roman youth once pitched camp, and indeed it seems likely, for one can see mounds, ditches, gates and all the other works for defending a camp.

11. Today went to Paradise, a garden very pleasant and beautiful to look on and rich in everything to delight us.

12. We saw a comedy and rope walkers.

13. We saw today a man eating fire.

14. We returned home today.

15. John Chapman told us that there was such a heavy fall of rain at Leicester that it had done much damage and drowned many sheep.

21. We caught fifty quite large fish.

25. Northampton market. Robert took Whitelegs and sold him for seven pounds.

AUGUST 1673

1. Today Mother set off with my sisters for Gloucester and I went as well. The intention was to visit Viscount Tracy, and when we arrived we were at once received with every mark of hospitality.

2. We went to Gloucester and heard the pneumatic organ there; they say it surpasses all others except the one at New College which we saw the other day. There is a spot in the cathedral where the smallest whisper can be easily heard at a very great distance. After dinner we went to Evening Prayers and then left the city, but darkness fell before we could reach Toddington, so we spent the night at an inn.

3/4. We went to Worcester.

10. We arrived at Baginton.

16. We arrived home. Mr Clerk informed us that Mr Mulso is dead. Lord Exeter sent us a haunch of venison. Henry Jones made a chest in the bedroom over the hall to put books in. They say that the Duke of York is going to marry the Duchess of Modena in September.

17. Cousin Spencer came to dinner. The wife of Sir William Fermor died in childbirth, but the daughter lived. We hear that Squire Digby is dead. Father received a letter from London with the news that we have engaged the Dutch Fleet and seized seven of their ships without loss to ourselves, though many are crippled and Edward Spragge has been killed.

18. Father went to see Mrs Mulso.

20. We hear that Harris has killed his fellow actor by accident on the stage. It was in the tragedy Macbeth. Harris, who took the part of Macduff, has to kill his friend Macbeth; in the fighting Macduff happened to pierce Macbeth's eye with his dagger and he fell dead at once, not even being able to speak the last words of his part, 'Farewell vain world, and what is worse, ambition.' Father and I went to Althorp, where he found the Countess of Sunderland's second youngest daughter dying of fever. Palmer told father that the Earl of Sunderland lost 20,000 pistols at play in a single night. On our return my sword fell out of the carriage, and as soon as I noticed it had gone I sent Holland and Perrot back to look for it, but they could not find it. The Papenburg, a Dutch ship returning from the East Indies, fell in

with our fleet and has been captured.

23. We took six ducks on our Houghton farms. Richard Porter took Tosser to Mr Freeman, who set his leg; then on my father's instructions he went to the crier, who proclaimed the loss of the sword. When this was done, a baker from Moulton, who followed the carriage, admitted that he had found it.

SEPTEMBER 1673

5. Mrs Collis hanged herself. Jonathan Tyler married Hilton's daughter.

6. Father, Mother and my sister Mary went to Lord Montagu's house to see Mr and Mrs Montagu, there were many lords and ladies there. We walked to Mr Ward's house.

8. Northampton market.

9. Mr Garrard and Wilmer came to dinner. Mr Palmer and Mr Shatto came too; they said they are expecting the Earl of Sunderland at Althorp tomorrow. Father and I went to visit Sir William Fermor and found there cousin Spencer.

18. We went to Brampton with Mr Bullivant to catch pike. We only took one small one, but had a very merry time at the miller's. Father was on his way back from Lord Sunderland's, who returned last night, and he found us there. He stayed at the mill for a while and then we returned home.

30. The harvest was gathered in and the boys raised their customary shouts.

The Diary of Thomas Isham of Lamport 1671-73, *translated by N. Marlow, selection of pages.*

Mr Pickwick visits The Saracen's Head, Towcester

Charles Dickens was a young reporter on the Morning Chronicle *and he used his experiences travelling around the country to write the* Pickwick Papers.

Returning from visiting Mr Winkle in Birmingham Sam Weller persuaded his master to stay overnight at the Saracen's Head, Towcester. Also arriving later was Mr Pott's arch rival Slurk of the

Independent. *The strong rivalry and amusing conversational exchange between Pott of the* Eatanswill Gazette *and Slurk of the* Independent *ended in comical but 'disgraceful public conduct.'*

'I say,' remonstrated Bob Sawyer, looking in at the coach window, as they pulled up before the door of the Saracen;s Head, Towcester, 'this won't do, you know.'

'Bless me!' said Mr Pickwick, just awaking from a nap, 'I'm afraid you're wet.'

'Oh you are, are you?' returned Bob. 'Yes, I am, a little that way. Uncomfortably damp, perhaps.'

Bob did look dampish, inasmuch as the rain was streaming from his neck, elbows, cuffs, skirts, and knees; and his whole apparel shone so with the wet, that it might have been mistaken for a full suit of prepared oilskin.

'I am rather wet,' said Bob, giving himself a shake, and casting a little hydraulic shower around, like a Newfoundland dog just emerged from the water.

'I think it's quite impossible to go on to-night,' interposed Ben.

'Out of the question, sir,' remarked Sam Weller, coming to assist in the conference; 'it's a cruelty to animals, sir, to ask 'em to do it. There's beds here, sir,' said Sam, addressing his master, 'everything clean and comfortable. Wery good little dinner, sir, they can get ready in half an hour - pair of fowls, sir, and a weal cutlet; French beans, 'taturs, tart, and tidiness. You'd better stop vere you are, sir, if I might recommend. Take adwice, sir, as the doctor said.'

The host of the Saracen's Head opportunely appeared at this moment, to confirm Mr Weller's statement relative to the accommodations of the establishment, and to back his entreaties with a variety of dismal conjectures regarding the state of the roads, the doubt of fresh horses being to be had at the next stage, the dead certainty of its raining all night, the equally mortal certainty of its clearing up in the morning, and other topics of inducement familiar to innkeepers.

'Well,' said Mr Pickwick; 'but I must send a letter to London by some conveyance, so that it maybe delivered the very first thing in the morning, or I must go forward at all hazards.'

The landlord smiled his delight. Nothing could be easier than for the gentleman to inclose a letter in a sheet of brown paper, and send it on, either by the mail or the night coach from Birmingham. If the gentleman were particularly anxious to have it left as soon as possible, he might write outside, 'To be delivered immediately,' which was sure to be attended to; 'or 'pay the bearer half-a-crown extra for instant delivery,' which was surer still.

'Very well,' said Mr Pickwick, 'then we will stop here.'

'Lights in the Sun, John; make up the fire; the gentlemen are wet!' cried the landlord. 'This way, gentlemen; don't trouble yourselves about the postboy now, sir. I'll send him to you when you ring for him, sir. Now, John, the candles.'

The candles were brought, the fire was stirred up, and a fresh log of wood thrown on. In ten minutes time, a waiter was laying the cloth for dinner, the curtains were drawn, the fire was blazing brightly, and everything looked (as everything always does, in all decent English inns) as if the travellers had been expected, and their comforts prepared, for days beforehand.

Mr Pickwick sat down at a side table, and hastily indited a note to Mr Winkle, merely informing him that he was detained by stress of weather, but he would certainly be in London next day; until when he deferred any account of his proceedings. This note was hastily made into a parcel, and despatched to the bar per Mr Samuel Weller.

Sam left it with the landlady, and was returning to pull his master's boots off, after drying himself by the kitchen fire, when, glancing casually through a half-opened door, he was arrested by the sight of a gentleman with a sandy head who had a large bundle of newspapers lying on the table before him, and was perusing the leading article of one with a settled sneer which curled up his nose and all his other features into a majestic expression of haughty contempt.

'Hallo!' said Sam, 'I ought to know that 'ere head and them features; the eye-glass, too, and the broad-brimmed tile! Eatanswill to vit or I'm a Roman.'

Sam was taken with a troublesome cough at once, for the purpose of attracting the gentleman's attention; the gentleman starting at the sound, raised his head and his eye-glass, and disclosed to view the profound and thoughtful features of Mr Pott, of the *Eatanswill Gazette*.

'Beggin your your pardon, Sir,' said Sam, advancing with a bow, 'my master's here, Mr Pott.'

'Hush, hush!' cried Pott, drawing Sam into the room, and closing the door, with a countenance of mysterious dread and apprehension.

'Wot's the matter, sir?' inquired Sam, looking vacantly about him.

'Not a whisper of my name,' replied Pott; 'this is a buff neighbourhood. If the excited and irritable populace knew I was here, I should be torn to pieces.'

'No! Vould you, sir?' inquired Sam.

'I should be the victim of their fury,' replied Pott. 'Now, young man, what of your master?'

'He's a stopping here to-night on his vay to town, with a couple of friends,' replied Sam.

'Is Mr Winkle one of them?' inquired Pott, with a slight frown.

'No, sir. Mr Vinkle stops at home now,' rejoined Sam. 'He's married!'

'Married!' exclaimed Pott, with frightful vehemence. He stopped, smiled darkly, and added, in a low, vindictive tone, 'It serves him right!'

Having given vent to this cruel ebullition of deadly malice and cold-blooded triumph over a fallen enemy, Mr Pott inquired whether Mr Pickwick's friends were 'blue?' Receiving a most satisfactory answer in the affirmative from Sam, who knew as much about the matter as Pott himself, he consented to accompany him to Mr Pickwick's room, where a hearty welcome awaited him. An agreement to club dinners together was at once made and ratified.

'And how are matters going on in Eatanswill?' inquired Mr Pickwick, when Pott had taken a seat near the fire, and the whole party had got their wet boots off, and dry slippers on. 'Is the *Independent* still in being?'

'The *Independent*, sir,' replied Pott, 'Is still dragging on a wretched and lingering career. Abhorred and despised by even the few who are cognizant of its miserable and disgraceful existence; stifled by the very filth it so profusely scatters; rendered deaf and blind by the exhalations of its own slime; the obscene journal, happily unconscious of its degraded state, is rapidly sinking beneath that treacherous mud which, while it seems to give it a firm standing with the low and debased classes of society, is nevertheless, rising above its detested head, and will speedily engulf it for ever.'

Having delivered this manifesto (which formed a portion of his last week's leader) with vehement articulation, the editor paused to take breath, and looked majestically at Bob Sawyer.

'You are a young man, sir,' said Pott.

Mr Bob Sawyer nodded.

'So are you, sir,' said Pott, addressing Mr Ben Allen.

Ben admitted the soft impeachment.

'And are both deeply imbued with those blue principles, which, so long as I live, I have pledged myself to the people of these kingdoms to support and to maintain?' suggested Pott.

'Why, I don't exactly know about that,' replied Bob Sawyer. 'I am'

'Not buff, Mr Pickwick,' interrupted Pott, drawing back his chair, 'your friend is not buff, sir?'

'No, no,' rejoined Bob, 'I'm a kind of plaid at present; a compound of all sorts of colours.'

'A waverer,' said Pott, solemnly, 'a waverer. I should like to show you a series of eight articles, sir, that have appeared in the *Eatanswill Gazette*. I think I may venture to say that you would not be long in establishing your opinions on a firm and solid blue basis, sir.'

'I dare say I should turn very blue, long before I got to the end of them,' responded Bob.

Mr Pott looked dubiously at Bob Sawyer for some seconds, and, turning to Mr Pickwick, said:

'You have seen the literary articles which have appeared at intervals in the *Eatanswill Gazette* in the course of the last three months, and which have excited such general - I may say such universal - attention and admiration?'

'Why,' replied Mr Pickwick, slightly embarrassed by the question, 'the fact is, I have been so much engaged in other ways, that I really have not had an opportunity of perusing them.'

'You should do so, sir,' said Pott, with a severe countenance.

'I will,' said Mr Pickwick.

'They appeared in the form of a copious review of a work on Chinese metaphysics, sir,' said Pott!

'Oh,' observed Mr Pickwick; 'from your pen, I hope?'

'From the pen of my critic, sir,' rejoined Pott with dignity.

'An abstruse subject I should conceive,' said Mr Pickwick.

'Very, sir,' responded Pott, looking intensely sage. 'He crammed for it, to use a technical but expressive term; he read up for the subject, at my desire, in the *Encyclopadia Britannica*.'

'Indeed!' said Mr Pickwick; 'I was not aware that that valuable work contained any information respecting Chinese metaphysics.'

'He read, sir,' rejoined Pott, laying his hand on Mr Pickwick's knee, and looking round with a smile of intellectual superiority, 'he read for metaphysics under the letter M, and for China under the letter C, and combined his information, sir!'

Mr Pott's features assumed so much additional grandeur at the recollection of the power and research displayed in the learned effusion in question, that some minutes elapsed before Mr Pickwick felt emboldened to renew the conversation; at length, as the Editor's countenance gradually relaxed into its customary expression of moral supremacy, he ventured to resume the discourse by asking:

'Is it fair to inquire what great object has brought you so far from home?'

'That object which actuates and animates me in all my gigantic labours, sir,' replied Pott, with a calm smile; 'my country's good.'

'I supposed it was some public mission,' observed Mr Pickwick.

'Yes, sir,' resumed Pott, 'it is.' Here, bending towards Mr Pickwick, he whispered in a deep hollow voice, 'A buff ball, sir, will take place in Birmingham to-morrow evening.'

'God bless me!' exclaimed Mr Pickwick.

'Yes, sir, and supper,' added Pott.

'You don't say so!' ejaculated Mr Pickwick.

Pott nodded portentously.

Now, although Mr Pickwick feigned to stand aghast at this disclosure, he was so little versed in local politics that he was unable to form an adequate comprehension of the importance of the dire conspiracy it referred to; observing which, Mr Pott, drawing forth the last number of the *Eatanswill Gazette*, and referring to the same, delivered himself of the following paragraph:

the conversation continues after an innocuous and long quotation from the Eatanswill Gazette *and the arrival at the inn of a new and interesting stranger . . .*

Bidding the other passengers good night, in a rather snappish manner, the stranger alighted. He was a shortish gentleman, with very stiff black hair cut in the porcupine or blacking-brush style, and

standing stiff and straight all over his head; his aspect was pompous
and threatening; his manner was peremptory; his eyes were sharp and
restless; and his whole bearing bespoke a feeling of great confidence
in himself, and a consciousness of immeasurable superiority over all
other people.

This gentleman was shown into the room originally assigned to the
patriotic Mr Pott; and the waiter remarked, in dumb astonishment at
the singular coincidence, that he had no sooner lighted the candles
than the gentleman, diving into his hat, drew forth a newspaper, and
began to read it with the very same expression of indignant scorn,
which, upon the majestic features of Pott, had paralysed his energies
an hour before. The man observed too, that whereas Mr Pott's scorn
had been roused by a newspaper headed *The Eatanswill Independent*,
this gentleman's withering contempt was awakened by a newspaper
entitled *The Eatanswill Gazette*.

'Send the landlord,' said the stranger.

'Yes, sir,' rejoined the waiter.

The landlord was sent, and came.

'Are you me landlord?' inquired the gentleman.

'I am, sir,' replied the landlord.

'Do you know me?' demanded the gentleman.

'I have, not that pleasure, sir,' rejoined the landlord.

'My name is Slurk,' said the gentleman.

The landlord slightly inclined his head.

'Slurk, sir,' repeated the gentleman, haughtily. 'Do you know me
now, man.'

The landlord scratched his head, looked at the ceiling, and at the
stranger, and smiled feebly.

'Do you know me, man?' inquired the stranger angrily.

The landlord made a strong effort, and at length replied: 'Well, sir,
I do not know you.'

'Great Heaven!' said the stranger, dashing his clenched fist upon the
table. 'And this is popularity!'

The landlord took a step or two towards the door; the stranger
fixing his eyes upon him, resumed.

'This,' said the stranger, 'this is gratitude for years of labour and
study on behalf of the masses. I alight wet and weary; no enthusiastic
crowds press forward to greet their champion; the churchbells are

silent; the very name elicits no responsive feeling in their torpid bosoms. It is enough,' said the agitated Mr Slurk, pacing to and fro, 'to curdle the ink in one's pen, and induce one to abandon their cause for ever.'

'Did you say brandy and water, sir?' said the landlord, venturing a hint.

'Rum,' said Mr Slurk, turning fiercely upon him. 'Have you got a fire anywhere?'

'We can light one directly, sir,' said the landlord.

'Which will throw out no heat until it is bed-time,' interrupted Mr Slurk. 'Is there anybody in the kitchen?'

Not a soul. There was a beautiful fire. Everybody had gone, and the house door was closed for the night.

'I will drink my rum and water,' said Mr Slurk, 'by the kitchen fire.' So, gathering up his hat and newspaper, he stalked solemnly behind the landlord to that humble apartment, and throwing himself on a settle by the fireside, resumed his countenance of scorn, and began to read and drink in silent dignity.

Now, some demon of discord, flying over the Saracen's Head at that moment, on casting down his eyes in mere idle curiosity, happened to behold Slurk established comfortably by the kitchen fire, and Pott slightly elevated with wine in another room; upon which the malicious demon, darting down into the last-mentioned apartment with inconceivable rapidity, passed at once into the head of Mr Bob Sawyer, and prompted him for his (the demon's) own evil purposes to speak as follows:

'I say, we've let the fire out. It's uncommonly cold after the rain, isn't it?'

'It really is,' replied Mr Pickwick, shivering.

'It wouldn't be a bad notion to have a cigar by the kitchen fire, would it?' said Bob Sawyer, still prompted by the demon aforesaid.

'It would be particularly comfortable, I think,' replied Mr Pickwick. 'Mr Pott, what do you say?'

Mr Pott yielded a ready assent; and all four travellers, each with his glass in his hand, at once betook themselves to the kitchen, with Sam Weller heading the procession to show them the way.

The stranger was still reading; he looked up and started. Mr Pott started.

'What's the matter?' whispered Mr Pickwick.

'That reptile!' replied Pott.

'What reptile?' said Mr Pickwick, looking about him for fear he should tread on some overgrown black beetle, or dropsical spider.

'That reptile,' whispered Pott, catching Mr Pickwick by the arm, and pointing towards the stranger. 'That reptile Slurk, of the *Independent*!'

'Perhaps we had better retire,' whispered Mr Pickwick.

'Never, sir,' rejoined Pott, pot-valiant in a double sense, 'never.'

With these words, Mr Pott took up his position on an opposite settle, and selecting one from a little bundle of newspapers, began to read against his enemy.

Mr Pott, of course, read the *Independent*, and Mr Slurk, of course, read the *Gazette*; and each gentleman audibly expressed his contempt of the other's compositions by bitter laughs and sarcastic sniffs; whence they proceeded to more open expressions of opinion, such as 'absurd,' 'wretched,' 'atrocity,' 'humbug,' 'knavery,' 'dirt,' 'filth,' 'slime,' 'ditch-water,' and other critical remarks of the like nature.

Both Mr Bob Sawyer and Mr Ben Allen had beheld these symptoms of rivalry and hatred, with a degree of delight which imparted great additional relish to the cigars at which they were puffing most vigorously. The moment they began to flag, the mischievous Mr Bob Sawyer, addressing Slurk with great politeness, said:

'Will you allow me to look at your paper, sir, when you have quite done with it!'

'You will find very little to repay you for your trouble in this contemptible thing sir,' replied Slurk, bestowing a Satanic frown on Pott.

'You shall have this presently,' said Pott, looking up, pale with rage, and quivering in his speech, from the same cause. Ha! ha! you will be amused with this fellow's audacity.

Terrific emphasis was laid upon this 'thing' and 'fellow;' and the faces of both editors began to glow with defiance.

'The ribaldry of this miserable man is despicably disgusting,' said Pott, pretending to address Bob Sawyer, and scowling upon Slurk.

Here, Mr Slurk laughed very heartily, and folding up the paper so as to get at a fresh column conveniently, said, that the blockhead really amused him.

'What an impudent blunderer this fellow is,' said Pott, turning from pink to crimson.

'Did you ever read any of this man's foolery, sir?' inquired Slurk, of Bob Sawyer.

'Never,' replied Bob; 'is it very bad?'

'Oh, shocking! shocking!' rejoined Slurk.

'Really! Dear me, this is too atrocious!' exclaimed Pott, at this juncture; still feigning to be absorbed in his reading.

'If you can wade through a few sentences of malice, meanness, falsehood, perjury, treachery, and cant,' said Slurk, handing the paper to Bob, 'you will, perhaps, be somewhat repaid by a laugh at the style of this ungrammatical twaddler.'

'What's that you said, sir?' inquired Mr Pott, looking up, trembling all over with passion.

'What's that to you, sir?' replied Slurk.

'Ungrammatical twaddler, was it, sir?' said Pott.

'Yes, sir, it was,' replied Slurk; 'and blue bore, sir, if you like that better; ha! ha!'

Mr Pott retorted not a word to this jocose insult, but deliberately folded up his copy of the *Independent*, flattened it carefully down, crushed it beneath his boot, spat upon it with great ceremony, and flung it into the fire.

'There, sir,' said Pott, retreating from the stove, 'and that's the way I would serve the viper who produces it, if I were not, fortunately for him, restrained by the laws of my country.'

'Serve him so, sir!' cried Slurk, starting up. 'Those laws shall never be appealed to by him, sir, in such a case. Serve him so, sir!'

'Hear! Hear!' said Sawyer.

'Nothing can be fairer,' observed Mr Ben Allen.

'Serve him so, sir!' reiterated Slurk, in a loud voice.

Mr Pott darted a look of contempt, which might have withered an anchor.

'Serve him so, sir!' reiterated Slurk, in a louder voice than before.

'I will not, sir,' rejoined Pott.

'Oh, you won't, won't you, sir?' said Mr Slurk, in a taunting manner; 'you hear this, gentlemen! He won't; not that he's afraid; oh, no! he won't. Ha! ha!'

'I consider you, sir,' said Mr Pott, moved by this sarcasm, 'I consider you a viper. I look upon you, sir, as a man who has placed himself beyond the pale of society, by his most audacious, disgraceful, and abominable public conduct. I view you, sir, personally and politically, in no other light than as a most unparalleled and unmitigated viper.'

The indignant *Independent* did not wait to hear the end of this personal denunciation; for, catching up his carpet-bag which was well stuffed with moveables, he swung it in the air as Pott turned away, and, letting it fall with a circular sweep on his head, just at that particular angle of the bag where a good thick hair-brush happened to be packed, caused a sharp crash to be heard throughout the kitchen, and brought him at once to the ground.

'Gentlemen,' cried Mr Pickwick, as Pott started up and seized the fire-shovel, 'gentlemen! Consider, for Heaven's sake - help - Sam - here - pray, gentlemen - interfere, somebody.'

Uttering these incoherent exclamations, Mr Pickwick rushed between the infuriated combatants just in time to receive the carpet-bag on one side of his body, and the fire-shovel on the other. Whether the representatives of the public feeling of Eatanswill were blinded by animosity, or (being both acute reasoners) saw the advantage of having a third party between them to bear all the blows, certain it is that they paid not the slightest attention to Mr Pickwick, but defying each other with great spirit, plied the carpet-bag and the fire-shovel most fearlessly. Mr Pickwick would unquestionably have suffered severely for his humane interference, if Mr Weller, attracted by his master's cries, had not rushed in at the moment, and, snatching up a meal sack, effectually stopped the conflict by drawing it over the head and shoulders of the mighty Pott, and clasping him tight round the shoulders.

'Take avay that 'ere bag from the t'other madman,' said Sam to Ben Allen and Bob Sawyer, who had done nothing but dodge round the group, each with a tortoise-shell lancet in his hand, ready to bleed the first man stunned. 'Give it up, you wretched little creetur, or I'll smother you in it.'

Awed by these threats, and quite out of breath, the *Independent* suffered himself to be disarmed; and Mr Weller, removing the extinguisher from Pott, set him free with a caution.

'You take yourselves off to bed quietly,' said Sam, 'or I'll put you both in it, and let you fight it out vith the mouth tied, as I vould a dozen sich, if they played these games. And you have the goodness to come this here vay, sir, if you please.'

Thus addressing his master, Sam took him by the arm, and led him off, while the rival editors were severally removed to their beds by the landlord, under the inspection of Mr Bob Sawyer and Mr Benjamin Allen; breathing, as they went away, many sanguinary threats, and making vague appointments for mortal combat next day. When they came to think it over, however, it occurred to them that they could do it much better in print, so they recommenced deadly hostilities without delay; and all Eatanswill rung with their boldness - on paper.

They had taken themselves off in separate coaches, early next morning, before the other travellers were stirring; and the weather having now cleared up, the chaise companions once more turned their faces to London.

The Posthumous Papers of The Pickwick Club, *Charles Dickens.*

The Charge of the Light Brigade

Sir Thomas Brudenall of Deene Park was made the first Earl of Cardigan in 1661 and it was the seventh Earl, James, who led and survived the Charge of the Light Brigade in 1854. The preserved head and tail of his charger, Ronald, can be seen in the house.

> Half a league half a league
> Half a league onward
> All in the valley of Death
> Rode the six hundred
> 'Forward the Light Brigade:
> Charge for the guns' he said
> Into the valley of Death
> Rode the six hundred
>
> 'Forward the Light Brigade!'
> Was there a man dismay'd?
> Not tho' the soldier knew
> Some one had blunder'd:
> Theirs not to make a reply,

Theirs not to reason why,
Theirs but to do and die,
Into the valley of Death
Rode the six hundred.

Cannon to right of them,
Cannon to left of them,
Cannon in front of them
Volley'd and thunder'd;
Storm'd at with shot and shell,
Boldly they rode and well,
Into the jaws of Death,
Into the mouth of Hell
Rode the six hundred.

Flash'd all their sabres bare,
Flash'd as they turn'd in air,
Sabring the gunners there,
Charging an army while
All the world wonder'd:
Plunged in the battery-smoke
Right thro' the line they broke;
Cossack and Russian
Reel'd from the sabre-stroke,
Shatter'd and sunder'd.
Then they rode back, but not
Not the six hundred.

Cannon to right of them,
Cannon to left of them,
Cannon behind them
Volley'd and thunder'd;
Storm'd at with shot and shell,
While horse and hero fell,
They that had fought so well
Came thro' the jaws of Death
Back from the mouth of Hell,
All that was left of them
Left of six hundred.

When can their glory fade?
O the wild charge they made!
All the world wonder'd.
Honour the charge they made!
Honour the Light Brigade,
Noble six hundred!

Alfred Tennyson 1809-1892.

Public Duty

Lady Knightley of Fawsley attended many public occasions, and surely would not have missed this one.

TUESDAY 18 OCTOBER 1887
EUSTON HALL, THETFORD

A long but interesting day. We drove over to Northampton to be present at the laying the first stone of the new wing of the Infirmary Northampton and Northamptonshire's own Jubilee memorial: Prince Albert Victor of Wales came from Althorp to perform the ceremony and there was the more excitement about it because the Socialists had threatened a counter demonstration with black flag etc. This however aroused such a strong feeling that they were obliged to abandon the idea, their platform being stormed on Sunday, and they themselves obliged to seek police protection. The result was that the Prince had a far more hearty reception than otherwise have been accorded him. The ceremony of laying the first stone was performed with full masonic honours, which always add very much to the picturesqueness and interest of the business. The Prince was very shy and nervous and read badly. Lord Euston, as Provincial Grand Master, read his address remarkably well. Lord Spencer as Grand Visitor of the Infirmary read an address from the Committee. Two hymns were sung and the Bishop pronounced the blessing, the only share in the ceremony that was allowed him, the Mayor being a strong Radical and dissenter. The Prince then went round the wards, the Spencers and ourselves with him, Rainald being President, and I was presented to my future sovereign who has the pretty manners of the rest of his family. He then drove away amid loud cheers and we started to walk down to the Town Hall but got into such a muddle were very glad to crawl into one of the Spencers' omnibuses with Lord Sandhurst. It was a curious sight to look at afterwards from the steps of the Town Hall, the surging mass of heads.

Politics and Society: The Journals of Lady Knightley of Fawsley 1885-1913, *Ed. Peter Gordon, Northampton Record Society, 1999, p 119.*

'The Road Will Last A Thousand Years'
The Opening of the New Motorway - M1

The building of the new motorway from London to Yorkshire was to answer all our long distance traffic problems, but what a disaster it was for the countryside and no one was spared, not even the traditional Northamptonshire 'Squires'. The Wakes of Courteenhall owned land through which a large section of the motorway was to be built.

If Courteenhall itself has remained largely unchanged over the centuries, it has, like so many other rural parts of Northamptonshire, been affected by external forces. The prime cause of change was the coming of the M1 motorway.

In February 1955, the Government of the day announced that Britain's first motorway, from London to Yorkshire, was to be built. The initial stage of some seventy miles would start from a point north of London, cross Bedfordshire and Buckinghamshire and terminate at Crick in Northamptonshire. By the following January it was revealed that at least a half of the one hundred objections registered with the Ministry of Transport had come from Northamptonshire. Professor Nikolaus Pevsner in his introduction to the volume on the county has written, 'It must be admitted that the soil of England is so closely and intimately worked and so subtly landscaped that the intrusion of the motorway was bound to be specially violent. It was for this reason that opposition to it remained for so long'.

The proposed motorway cut diagonally across the Courteenhall Estate with an intersection where the A508 crossed the M1 at Junction 15. In 1957 the Estate was warned that a compulsory acquisition order was being prepared by the Ministry of Transport, and on 27 February 1958 the order itself was received: later that year, Major Wake was taken in the contractor's helicopter to survey the route of the motorway.

A remarkable feature of the project was the speed with which it was built. Sir Owen Williams and Partners were briefed in 1951, but work on the M1 did not go ahead until 24 March 1958. By September the following year - a period of eighteen months - the road was open from London to Crick. The scale of the operation was very impressive: it involved five thousand men, five million pounds worth of machinery and twelve thousand maps. Working day and night, the contractors, John Laing and Son Ltd., surfaced two and a half million square yards of motorway, carried one hundred and thirty two bridges over or under existing roads, railways, canals and footpaths, and built a service station every twelve miles.

The compensation which the Estate received from the Ministry of Transport in November 1963 for the conveyance of the Courteenhall land was £15,246, with an additional sum of £1,403 for interest accrued. A separate cheque for the derisory sum of £3 13s. 4d. was sent by the Ministry 'for inconvenience suffered'. Five of the seven Courteenhall farms - East Lodge Farm, Grange Farm, Home Farm, Wards Farm and West Lodge Farm - were affected by the motorway. Accommodation works carried out included the building of a bridge for the drive to East Lodge Farm, where two cattle grids were built. Six other bridges were erected on the Estate, all existing footpaths and bridle roads being preserved.

The building of the M1 created many problems for Courteenhall. Two streams which now took the surface water from the motorway had to be regularly cleaned. Piped water had to be connected to several fields and existing power lines had to be altered. When the cuttings were being excavated, the top soil was dumped in adjoining fields. Eighteen months later when it was cleared away, some of the original soil disappeared too. The design of the early bridges over the motorway was unpleasing as they were built at speed; subsequent motorway bridges are of better design. The road itself, altogether six lanes in width, has large embankments on each side of it. No consideration was paid by the Ministry of Transport at this time for the privacy of landowners along the motorway, and no landscaping was undertaken. At first, it was contemplated that as Courteenhall House was now completely visible from the M1, it would provide a pleasing view for the passing motorist. There was also the problem of the noise generated by the constant stream of traffic day and night. To alleviate these problems, in the last twenty five years, Sir Hereward has planted belts and spinneys, largely of evergreen trees. The appearance of the Courteenhall Estate has thus been totally changed. The names given to the spinneys, containing approximately a quarter of a million trees, have mainly Wake associations, consisting either of place names, such as Bourne, Clevedon, Waltham and Alamein, or the names of the children and grandchildren.

At a lunch given at Newport Pagnell on 30 September 1959 to celebrate the completion of the first section of the M1, Sir Owen Williams, the consulting engineer, anticipated that 'the road would last for about a thousand years'. This optimistic estimate was dampened a month later by the main contractors on the day of the official opening of the M1, 2 November, who stated, 'There is no guarantee that settlement and cracking will not occur'. With between sixteen and seventeen thousand vehicles using the motorway on the first day, it was not surprising that within thirty six hours it was reported that the hard shoulder had collapsed at one point under the weight of a heavy lorry.

One consequence of the motorway has been the heavy increase in traffic in the area, both on the road itself and those leading off it at Junction 15 past Courteenhall; bypasses, road widening and extra exits and entrances to and from the motorway are the only means of alleviating the problem. Recently it has been stated, 'It (the M1) was destined to give new emphasis to the "At-the-Crossroads-of-Britain" image of Northampton, highlight its role as an ideal distribution centre and compensate for its decline as a manufacturing town'. The building of the motorway has indeed doubled the size of Northampton during the past thirty years, and has led to the expansion of nearly all the other towns and villages in the County, and the building of Milton Keynes to the south.

The Wakes of Northamptonshire, *Peter Gordon, Northamptonshire Libraries and Information Service, 1992, p 348, 352.*

7 · ROYALTY

Many will be aware of Diana, Princess of Wales' associations with Althorp, but Northamptonshire has had royal connections since as early as the Anglo-Saxons.

Early Care for the Needy

The charter granting Northampton a medieval hospital was undated, but it seems to have been granted between 1154, Henry II's accession to the throne, and 1162 when Thomas Becket, the Chancellor resigned.

Henry, King of England, Duke of Normandy and Aquitaine, and Count of Anjou, to the Bishop of Lincoln, and all barons, justiciars, sheriffs, ministers, and all his faithful subjects of Northantscire (Northamptonshire) greeting. Know all that I have granted and confirmed to the brethren of the hospital of St John's of Northampton, whatever they have reasonably and justly acquired, and whatever they shall justly and reasonably acquire in gifts, accatis (acquisitions) and alms. Wherefore I will firmly command that they hold and enjoy all the aforesaid possessions, well, peacefully, freely and quietly within and without the borough, in wood and in plain, in highways and in by-ways, in waters and mills and in all places, together with all liberties, free customs, lands, etcetera. and that which pertains to them; and I forbid anyone hereafter to do them injury or wrong.

Witnesses Thomas the Chancellor, Henry of Essex, the Constable, and Joscelyne de Baillol, at Mindestud in the Forest.

Extract taken from A History of the Hospital of St John Northampton, K. Cushing.

Joan, The Fair Maid of Kent

Although there is no known link with the legendary 'Hereward the Wake', the famous Wakes can trace their roots to Geoffrey Wac, a Norman born during the 11th century. The family has associations throughout the country and it was probably during the 13th century that they became established in Blisworth and four centuries later at Courteenhall. Joan Wake, known as 'The Fair Maid of Kent', lost her first husband in 1360 and as a widow of 32 with three children and famed for her beauty eventually married the Black Prince, and was mother to Richard II, who was crowned King in July 1371 at the age of ten. The wooing of Joan by the Black Prince is recorded in a French chronicle.

She showed herself a lady of great subtlety and wisdom. For the Prince was enchanted with her and said to her, 'Ah, my dear cousin, is it the case that you refuse to marry any of my friends in spite of your great beauty? Although you and I are of the same lineage, there is no lady under heaven that I hold so dear as you.' Thereon the Prince became greatly enamoured of the Countess and the Countess commenced to weep like a subtle and far-seeing woman. And then the Prince began to comfort her and kiss her passionately, grievously distressed at her tears, and said to her, 'I have spoken to you on behalf of one of the most chivalrous Knights of England and one of the most honourable of men.' Madame the Countess replied in tears to the Prince, 'Ah, Sir, before God do you not talk to me thus. For I have given myself to the most chivalrous Knight under heaven, and for love of him it is, that before God I will never marry again for as long as I live. For it is impossible that I should have to my husband and my love for him

parts me from all men: it is my intention never to marry'. The Prince was extremely curious to know who was the most chivalrous Knight in the world, and pressed the Countess to tell him. But the Countess the more she saw him aflame, the more she begged him to make no further enquiry and said to him. 'Before God, my very dear Lord, by His agony, by the sweet Virgin Mother, suffer it to be so'. To make a long story short, the Prince told her that if she did not tell him who was the most chivalrous Knight in the world, he would make him his deadly enemy. Then the Countess said to him, 'My dear and indomitable lord it is you, and for love of you that I will never have any other Knight by my side.' The Prince, greatly amazed by the love of the Countess, replied, 'My Lady, I also vow to God that as long as you live never will I have any other woman save you to my wife'.
Chronique des Quatres Premiers Valois.

Royal Miracles

King Henry VI at his coronation was anointed with a miraculous oil, which is said to have given credence to his shaky pretensions to the throne. Northamptonshire is thought to have had six miracles, all posthumously performed by King Henry VI.

A mad woman in a Northamptonshire village called Ashby Leger was miraculously cured through the invocation by the faithful of the blessed King Henry. She was the wife of a certain Geoffrey Brawnston. July 23rd 1486.

A young girl called Alice Parkyn was working in a sandpit, digging out sand, when a huge weight of it fell over and around her. She was delivered from instant death by heart-felt invocation of the blessed King Henry. This happened not far from a town called Brawnston in the county of Northampton. Dated 1484.

A young boy of six months called George Trevagnes, was caught and hanged to death in his own cradle, but when his mother lamented much and cried continually to the blessed King Henry he awoke and drew breath again suddenly. Brackley 1491.

The child, Knox enlarges, was holding a rattle from which hung a cord. While the mother was asleep, the child, by entangling itself with the cord, was hanged by it. The mother awoke to find it dead, but by prayers and the bent coin it was restored to life.

A man had lost the use of his legs but managed to go to Windsor on horseback. Miraculously recovered, he returned home on foot. Middleton Cheney.

A little boy called Edmund Brown was drowned in a pool full of dirty water and after a long space of time recovered the breath of life as before when the most devote King Henry was involved. Higham Ferrers.

Fotheringhay's Sad and Distinguished Visitor

Fotheringhay and the Castle will always be associated with Mary, Queen of Scots – beheaded in it in 1587. The story of Mary is one of the great tragedies of British history. Born a Catholic and crowned Queen of Scotland aged nine months in 1543, much of her life was surrounded by plotting and intrigue. Finally she was forced to abdicate and throw herself at the mercy of her cousin, Elizabeth I. After spending twenty years under house arrest, she was brought south to Fotheringhay, accused of plotting to overturn Elizabeth and charged with treason. The outcome of the trial was never in doubt and in 1586 she was sentenced to death and executed on February 8th 1587. Mary, however, had previously given birth to the future King James. Here, in extracts from a rare manuscript, Mary recounts a strange vision prior to the birth and her thoughts immediatley after the reading of her death warrant.

The time of my delivery drawing near, I retired, by the advice of my Privy Council to the Castle of Edinburgh. When walking one evening about twilight on the ramparts thereof, I observed my walk often crossed by an uncouth figure: alarmed at this circumstance, and suspecting treachery, I flew immediately to my chamber, where I spent the night in a state of sleepless anxiety, revolving in my mind a hundred causes for the singular object I had beheld, but without being able to fix on any thing. Reflection served to recruit my scattered senses, and regardless of the phantom, although it frequently crossed my way, I continued my nocturnal walks on the ramparts: at length, one evening, being grown more familiar with the sight, I halted, and looking more earnestly at the phantom, perceived it bore the resemblance of a woman bent nearly double, whose pale and distorted countenance, together with something which I heard it mutter, reminded me of the Weird Sisters I had so often heard of. The phantom looked on me at this moment with a fixed and vacant glare; and whilst I shuddered with affright, breaking silence, addressed me thus:

'Hail, rival of Elizabeth, hail, Queen of Scotland, thou shalt be the mother of a King, who Phoenix like, shall rise upon thy ashes; but beware of courtly wiles and crafty knaves, who plot thy sure destruction; shun the English shore, for there the root of all thy woes is sowed;' so saying, the phantom vanished, and I retired to my chamber trembling with affright, where I was soon after taken ill, and the next morning delivered of my only son, who was afterwards christened by the name of James.

The narrative ends with Mary Queen of Scots preparing for her execution: 'The commissioners have been, they have just read my death warrant, and to-morrow Gracious Heaven! Elizabeth sheds the blood of one who never injured her, I die to expiate faults, not of my own committing. Oh! my son, never shall I see more a presence which could soothe me midst affliction - but, hark, they come - I'll hide these papers - may future ages read and pity me - the fatal moment is arrived - have mercy - Heaven.'

The manuscript ended but an annexed paper had been written by an observer:

The morning fixed for the execution being arrived, the, ill-fated queen was conducted into the hall, where she found the block and every necessary appendage for her execution completed. She viewed the terrific scene with unconcern; and falling on her knees repeated a prayer in Latin, then kissing the crucifix, she offered up a prayer for the prosperity of, Elizabeth and the English nation, this done, she spent a few minutes in silent devotion, then taking leave of her domestics, she laid her head on the block, when it was immediately severed from her body, the hair of which had turned grey through the excess of sorrow she had experienced.

Thus fell the Royal Captive of Fotheringhay Castle; her fate even regretted by her enemies, leaving an indelible stain on the character of Elizabeth; who dying soon after, the crown devolved to James the Sixth, fully proving the truth of the phantom's assertion, that he should Phoenix like, rise from the ashes of an ill-fated mother.

Supplied from a rare manuscript published in 1808 by Tegg and Castleman.

He Buried Two Queens

One of the County's most famous epitaphs is to Robert Scarlett, the long-lived, (he died at 98 years of age), sexton of Peterborough Cathedral. He buried two queens – Katherine of Aragon in 1536 and Mary Queen of Scots' first interment in 1587. His portrait, which also shows the tools of his trade – a shovel, pickaxe and skull, hangs in Peterborough Cathedral.

You see old Scarlett's picture stand on high;
But at your feet there doth his body lye.
His gravestone doth his age and death-time show,
His office by these tokens you may know.
Second to none for strength and sturdy Limme,
A scare-babe mighty voice, with visage grimme;
He had interr'd two Queens within this place,
And this townes Householders in his life's space
Twice over; But at length his own time came,
What hee for others did, for him the same
Was done. No doubt his Soul doth live for aye
In heaven, though his body clad in clay.

Chalybeate for the Royals

King Charles I and his Queen, Henrietta, visited Wellingborough on several occasions (1628, 1637) to 'take the waters' of the Red Well. Wellingborough, a market town, has a twentieth century estate and schools called Redwell.

A royal pair once with their kingly court,
Visited Redwell and drank the healing stream,
Pitching their tents in the warm summer beam;
The courtiers with the pair, a noble sort,
A high born people to their sovereign brought,
Their services, their loving, loyal theme;
A hearty sacrifice, unselfish scheme,
That courtiers give to kings as courtiers ought.
The Redwell medicinal stream would have made
A famous spring to all posterity;
Visited by a monarch and courtiers free;
His countenance giving the most active aid.
A royal prerogative might have been
Ours to all time if we had but foreseen.

John Askham, Northamptonshire Notes and Queries, *Vol IV, 1892.*

Lady Knightley's Grief

TUESDAY 22 JANUARY 1901
FAWSLEY

Will ever be a sad day in the memories of all Englishmen and women now living, for on this day it has pleased Our Heavenly Father to take to Himself our Sovereign Lady, Queen VIctoria. The account on Sunday in the Westminster Gazette was most alarming, and I felt then as I knelt in church that I was listening to that name in the prayers for the last time. Monday came a slight rally, which by this morning's news was maintained, but tonight we hear that she passed away about 6.15. It is a blessed ending to a beautiful life, no long, lingering illness, no loss of mental faculties to the last, showing that wonderful sympathy which has so endeared her to her people. The accounts of the intense feeling aroused throughout the Empire are quite marvellous. It is one of the many things which if one did not see one would not believe. The German Emperor has come over, which pleases us all.

Politics and Society, The Journals of Lady Knightley of Fawsley 1885-1913,
P. Gordon, Northamptonshire Record Society, 1999, p 339.

A Modern Tragedy, Diana, Princess of Wales

Much has been written about Diana, Princess of Wales, and her tragic death in Paris on 31 August 1997. Perhaps two powerful and emotional readings at her funeral summarise feelings and give thought and thanks for her life.

The Dean of Westminster read The Bidding.
'We are gathered here in Westminster Abbey to give thanks for the life of Diana, Princess of Wales, to commend her soul to almighty God, and to seek His comfort for all who mourn. In her life, Diana profoundly influenced this nation and the world. She kept company with Kings and Queens, with Princes and Presidents, but we especially remember her humane concerns and how she met individuals and made them feel significant. Let us re-dedicate to God the work of those many charities that she supported; let us commit ourselves anew to caring for others.'

Following the hymn, 'I Vow to Thee, My Country', Sarah McCorquodale, Diana's elder sister, gave a reading:

> If I should die and leave you here awhile,
> Be not like others, sore undone, who keep
> Long vigils by the silent dust, and weep.
> For my sake - turn again to life and smile,
> Nerving thy heart and trembling hand to do
> Something to comfort other hearts than thine.
> Complete those dear unfinished tasks of mine
> And I, perchance, may therein comfort you.

8 · THE HUSTINGS

The Prayer used by both Houses of Parliament

Sir Christopher Yelverton, now buried in Easton Maudit church, whilst a Member of Parliament for Northampton in the sixteenth century, became the Speaker, and composed and read daily the prayer which is still used in both houses at the beginning of each sitting.

Almighty God, by whom alone Kings reign and Princes decree justice and from whom alone cometh all counsel, wisdom and understanding; we thine unworthy servants here gathered together in Thy Name do most humbly beseech Thee to send down Thy Heavenly Wisdom from above, to direct and guide us in all our consultations: And grant that, we having Thy fear always before our eyes, and laying aside all private interests, prejudices and partial affections, the result of our counsels may be the glory of Thy Blessed Name, the maintenance of true Religion and Justice, the safety, honour and happiness of the Queen, the public wealth, peace and tranquillity of the Realm, and the uniting and knitting together of the hearts of all persons and estates within the same, in true Christian Love and Charity one towards another, through Jesus Christ our Lord and Saviour.

The Houses of Parliament – An Illustrated Guide to the Palace of Westminster, 1965.

Justices of the Peace 1361

*The following extracts are from the translation of the Act of 34
Edward III making the appointment of J.P.'s throughout the realm.
Their job being to enforce the law and punish offenders.*

A Statute Made In The Parliament House At Westminster

These are the things which our Lord the King, the Prelates, Lords
and Commons have ordained in this present Parliament, the Sunday
next before the Feast of the Conversion of St Paul.

First, that in every County of England shall be assigned for the
keeping of the Peace, one Lord, and with him three or four of the most
worthy in the County, with some learned in law, and they shall have
power to restrain the offenders, rioters, and all other barators, and to
pursue, arrest, take and chastise them according to their trespass or
offences, and cause them to be imprisoned and duly punished
according to the law and customs of the realm . . . And to hear and
determine at the King's suit all manner of felonies and trespasses done
in the same county . . .

*The list of the Justices appointed to the first Commission of the Peace
in Northamptonshire, dated 15th December 1361 was:*

Henry Grene	Thomas Wake of Blisworth
Robert de Thorp	John Knyvet
John de Lyouns	Henry, Duke of Lancaster
Thomas de Preston	Robert de Holand
Nicholas de Thenford	John de Verdoun
John de Haruwedon (Harrowden)	

Calendar of Patent Rolls, 1361-64, p 66. *Statute translated from French.*

An Untimely End

*Violence was commonplace in medieval England and William
Tresham, Lord of the Manor at Sywell and four times speaker of the
House of Commons under Henry VI, was no exception.*

Tresham 'was at his owen place' at Sywell (Northants) on 22
September 1450 purposing to 'mete and speke' with the Duke of

Yorke who had written to him. That day 'toward nyght' a Rutland esquire, Simon Norwich, a group of 'yeoman' of Beds and Northants with some from Wales, sent one of their number – a Kislingbury man – to Tresham, to pretend that he wanted him to be his 'good maister, in a feigned suit he had with the Duke. This was in order to learn the time of Tresham's departure. When this information was gained the conspirators assembled a gang of over 160 armed men at a place called Thorpeland Close in Multon, which was some four miles from Sywell on the road to Northampton. There they waited for Tresham who came by early in the following morning 'seiying matyns of oure Lady', and out of their ambush they set upon and killed him and robbed him of a collar of the royal livery, a chain of gold, his signet, certain jewels, £20 in money, and his horse. They also severely wounding the ex-speaker's son, Thomas, who was accompanying his father, and robbed him too.

Northamptonshire Past and Present, 1957, Vol II, J.S. Roskell, p 201.

To The Working Classes

A handbill protesting against the new Poor Laws in 1841 and urging the election of a candidate who supports the poor cause.

The election is in your own hands. Pity those that are suffering within the workhouse prison from want or sickness, age or sorrow. Think of them, and do not, for money or drink, oh! do not vote for any member, or any supporter of a cruel Workhouse Government. To vote either Smith or for Currie would be to vote your poorer neighbours into the Bastile first, and yourselves into it afterwards!

If any person desires you to vote for Workhouse Candidate, refuse at once. If you do not at once refuse, at all events take a little time to consider it. During that time ask your wives what they, who may one day become widows, would wish. Can they wish to end their days in the Bastile? Ask your children what they, who may one day become orphans, would wish. Can they wish to live, if living it can be called, in a Bastile?

One word more. Ask yourselves what you, as well as they, are likely to wish, should you live to become aged or sick.

Think of this before you give a vote to a poor man's enemy, against the poor man's friend. Think of all this now that your poor countryman everywhere have their eyes upon your votes, hoping that you will elect the poor man's friend.

May you come to a humane and Christian conclusion. Thus may the working man's election prove the working man's blessing. Thus may Sir Henry Willoughby be rewarded for all his past resistance to the workhouse system by the confidence of the poor. And thus may Sir Henry Willoughby be enabled in Parliament again to prove himself the poor man's friend.

Electors! Forget not the poor!

Bradlaugh For Northampton!

Charles Bradlaugh stood in the 1868 election in Northampton and although not successful he built up a following which resulted in him being elected in 1880. During his first campaign the song 'Bradlaugh for Northampton' was written by James Wilson and set to music by John Lowry. The verses are currently carved around the Bradlaugh monument in Abington Square, Northampton.

Electors of Northampton, work!
The day will soon be here,
When you will have to give your votes,
And give them without fear;
For freedom's battle ne'er was won
By cowards in the past,
Nor can it ever be sustained
By men who fear the blast.

Then toil, men, toil in freedom's cause,
Rest not content with vain applause.
Humanity needs better laws–
To win these we'll send Bradlaugh!

'Tis not to tread your churches down,
Nor chapels built by men,
Nor hinder earnest worshippers
On mountain or in glen;

But to give freedom to each thought
That swells the brain of man,
Religious liberty for all,
No State Church in our plan.

Then toll, men, toll in freedom's cause,
Rest not content with vain applause.
The nation needs far better laws–
To Win these we'll send Bradlaugh!

'Tis not to rob rich lords of lands,–
Oppress as they would you,
Nor property make insecure,
To feed a lawless few;
But to make way for those to rise,
Who hard yet humbly toil,
And give to all some interest
In Nature's gift, the soil.

Then toil, men, toil in freedom's cause,
Rest not content with vain applause.
Our starving poor cry 'BETTER LAWS';
Then, hail success to Bradlaugh!

Some cowards cry out, 'Heresy!'
Beware! My fellow men,–
That cry's been raised, so hist'ry says,
'Gainst Britain's noblest men,
Say, is he manly, is he true?
Is he for justice strong?
And will he labour good to do?
Then echo in your song–

We'll toil, we'll toil in freedom's cause,
Nor rest content with vain applause,
But fight determined for just laws–
And make our member, Bradlaugh!
The Late Charles Bradlaugh MP, Campion, 1894

The following three extracts from Lady Knightley's diary indicate not only her support for the women's suffrage movement and her wish to achieve the vote by constitutional, not militant means, but also her support for her husband as a Member of Parliament.

Suffragettes

WEDNESDAY 27 APRIL 1892
FIRLE

Another lovely day. I drove my darling into Lewes on his way to London to vote in favour of Women's Suffrage. He has just (11 p.m.) returned, well pleased with the division. We were only beat by 23; which, considering that Mr. Gladstone wrote a pamphlet against us and that a tremendous whip was issued signed by Sir. H. James, Mr. Chamberlain, Lord R. Churchill. Lord George Hamilton, Sir M.W. Ridley, Sir Walter Barttelot and other equally weighty names, was most satisfactory. The fact is it is undoubtedly gaining ground in the country though not in society and it will come in time. A disgraceful riot last night at a Women's Suffrage meeting at St. James's Hall. I can't make out the ins and outs of it.

Election Fever

FRIDAY 27 NOVEMBER 1885
FAWSLEY

Was the long looked for day of polling. Rainald and I drove down to Badby after luncheon, which was a mass of blue and full of enthusiasm. Then he voted for himself while I waited outside and felt, for the first time personally, the utter anomaly of my not having a vote while Joe Bull has! We drove on to Daventry and Welton where there comparatively little excitement but our friends seemed quite content. And we have good reports from Byfield, Maidford and Weedon. Tomorrow will be tremendously exciting for not only this but 37 other county seats are decided today: if they do but follow the boroughs our triumph is secured! All Europe is watching and as one of the papers remarks, the vote of the English agricultural labourer will seriously affect the Egyptian fellaheen. Meanwhile the poor little King of Spain is dead and Servia and Bulgaria have lighted a blaze in the over inflammable East.

... and the Results

SATURDAY 28 NOVEMBER 1885

CLARIDGE'S HOTEL

Almost the most exciting day I ever spent in my life. We drove over in the brougham to Towcester and I was deposited at the Pomfret Arms while Rainald went down to the Town Hall where the votes were being counted. Nearly an hour elapsed and I was beginning to wonder very much at hearing nothing when the maid came up and said Mr. Norman had come for me. I went down and found the Superintendent of Police with the message; 'Sir Rainald is in but by very few, only about 50'. And we had hoped for 500!! I went down to the Town Hall and waited a long time while the votes were all counted again, Sir Maurice appeared and was very civil saying, 'Let me be the first to congratulate you'. Then Rainald came up and finally the poll was declared: Knightley 4074, FitzGerald 4012, majority 62. A crowd of men and boys had collected, evidently of Radical propensities, who cheered at the window: they would not let a word that Rainald said be heard but listened to Sir Maurice when he expressed his intention of fighting and winning another day. So he may as far as we are concerned for nothing will induce Rainald ever to stand again. Well, he will carry his bat out and with the proud conviction of having saved the seat, which no one else could. Our friends were very nervous and fidgety and wanted us not to walk away but we insisted on doing so being well hooted and groaned at though our supporters cheered us well when we got back to the inn. We went straight to Blisworth, and came on here a good deal shaken and tired with it all. However, it is all right though it will have no moral effect as we had hoped. Varying fortune in the other county constituencies: Lord Percy beat by 1400, Hertfordshire, Berkshire, Bucks, Devon, Essex, Cheshire more or less right. But certainly we have been living in a fool's paradise. Towcester and Brackley districts must have been much worse than we had any idea of. Tiny says I have won it for him.

Politics and Society, The Journals of Lady Knightley of Fawsley 1885-1913, P. Gordon, 1999, NRS, p 192, 81, 82.

9 · CONFRONTATION

Military Activity on the Racecourse

St. Matthew's church looks over the old Racecourse and dominates the surounding area. During the First World War the parishioners gave support and comfort to the billeted servicemen.

The close proximity of St. Matthew's parish to the great war camp on the Northampton Racecourse made the church a centre for military religious observances. To view the Racecourse from the top of the Church tower when any manoeuvres were in progress was like looking down at an actual battlefield; occasionally, when there was a route march, the road past the church was filled with guns, horses and men in ceaseless stream from 7.00 a.m. until midday. The whole parish was a barracks, almost every house having its contingent of billeted men. The Welsh Division (wonderful singers they were!), the Gloucestershire and Warwickshire Regiments worshipped at St. Matthew's Services on Sundays succeeded each other almost hourly, one thousand men marching in as another thousand left: sometimes as many as five military bands were stationed outside.

There were many Catholic Churchmen among the soldiers, especially in the Warwickshire Regiment which had many parishioners from St. Alban's, Birmingham, who found St. Matthew's a spiritual home. It was no uncommon thing to see a considerable number of men in khaki waiting to make their confession after the Saturday Evensong, or, when no server happened to be present at the daily Eucharist, to see a soldier leaving his place in the chapel to serve. Of course, many of the choir and servers of the church had gone, some, alas, never to return.

The particular field of church work which most felt the war conditions was the Sunday School; the effect upon that for the time being was disastrous. The boys were undisciplined in the absence of their fathers; the girls were naturally excited and reckless. Mothers, with three or four soldiers in their houses to be provided for, found it impossible to get their younger children ready for school, and seemed to lose all control over their elder girls. A Girls' Bible Class of nearly eighty members dwindled away altogether; the number of children in the (Sunday) School lessened by several hundreds. The loss was inevitable, and no one could wonder at it while the Racecourse provided such absorbing sights. To the teachers the work during those years was heart-breaking indeed; many tears were shed over the apparently useless efforts. It was a really hard struggle to hold on in faith that some day the former conditions of order and discipline would be restored.

The Centenary History of St Matthew's Church and Parish, Northampton, M. Harrison, 1993, Pentland Press, p 48, 49.

The Battle of Naseby

The Civil War, sometimes called 'The Great Rebellion', was the result of a quarrel between King Charles I and the English Parliament over who should govern the country. Charles I ruled without Parliament between 1629 and 1640, but when Parliament was re-called in 1640 there was again conflict between the two. Civil War broke out in 1642 when the armies of the Royalists (Cavaliers) and the Parliamentarians (Roundheads) first clashed at Nottingham. During the next three years battles were won and lost until the decisive Battle of Naseby. This unique account was found on a rare unsigned engraving and attributed to an artist of the period, and ends with the King's retreat.

This Battle which gave the fatal turn to the Kings Affairs happen'd on the 14th June 1645 the first charge was given by the right wing of horse and foot commanded by Prince Rupert, and his Brother, who board down all before them, the left wing and the Northern Horse enraging Cromwell and the Enemies right wing against odds of numbers and the advantage Ground were put to Flight. The King at the head of his reserves of Horse was even ready to charge those which pursued his left wing which might have recover'd the misfortune when on a Sudden such a panic fear seized on them and they all ran near of a quarter of a mile without stopping, which happen'd upon common accident. For the Scotch Earl of Carnworth on a Sudden laid his hand on ye King's bridle, flying out with 2 or 3 Oaths, will You go upon your Death in an Instant! and before his Majesty understood what he would have turn'd his Horse round, upon which a word runs through the Troops, March to the Right which unfortunately led them from charging the Enemy and assisting their own Men, and caused them all to turn their Horses, and ride upon the Spur as if every man was to see for himself. After this Disorder the King not being able to prevail with his Troops to rally and charge the enemy He retreated as well as He could and left Fairfax entire master of the Field.

Northamptonshire Notes and Queries, *Volume II, 1886, p 6.*

Unhappy Militia

April 19th 1672. War being proclaimed and begun against Holland, many soldiers are being pressed in town and country. Today thirty-three men passed by our village on their way to London, to fight the Dutch, and ten armed men, horse and foot, were assigned as their escort. One of the escort was Abraham, the brother of Edward Freeman. When they arrived near Brixworth they rested on the grass and had dinner brought from the town, bread and cheese with plenty of strong ale. They are being kept away from towns as far as possible, in case they desert up narrow alleys or lurk in hiding.

The Diary of Thomas Isham of Lamport, *translated by N. Marlow, originally written 1671-73.*

Lynching 1322

Murders were common place in medieval England, but often justice was ultimately seen to be had, if not legally!

On a day in March 1322, Henry Felip and his son were heading home to Stoke Bruerne from Northampton. At Courteenhall they were waylaid by six robbers. Felip quickly thrust his coins into his son's hand. "Take the money; Go and get help." He turned to face the robbers, and his son ran round them out of their reach. At nearby Courteenhall young Felip raised the hue and cry. It was the law that all who heard a cry of alarm, when a crime was committed or discovered, were bound to give assistance, without delay. It was the medieval equivalent of dialling 999.

Followed by willing Courteenhall men, young Felip ran back to the scene of the incident. Too late! His father lay dead on the ground. The grief-stricken young man had to decide, quickly, whether to stay with his father's corpse, or go with the others in an attempt to catch up with the killers, identify them and apprehend them. In the distance, figures could be seen running towards Northampton. His father's murderers had to be caught.

After a chase, five of the six miscreants were overtaken and arrested. The sixth, turned off the road to the right, heading towards the church of Wootton. When Felip and some of his helpers arrived, the robber was inside and safe from capture.

The law of sanctuary gave full protection to any fugitive, however serious the crime he or she had committed, so long as certain procedures were properly carried out. The punishment for violating sanctuary was severe, so Felip and his companions could do no more than stand helplessly at the door. Only a few days before this, two soldiers from Cold Ashby had killed the man who had recruited them by shoving a lance through his body.

They had then gone into Cold Ashby Church and claimed sanctuary, thus escaping punishment for their crime.

The next step for the robber in Wootton Church was to confess his guilt to the Coroner. Richard Luvell, of Farthingstone, Coroner, was duly sent for, and arrived on Wednesday 24th March, with witnesses from Wootton and the three nearest villages.

The fugitive gave his name, John of Ditchford. He confessed that he had participated in the murder of Henry Felip at Courteenhall.

'Do you abjure the realm?' asked the Coroner.

'What does that mean?'

'You have to agree to leave the country and never return. If you come back you, can be executed for your crime.'

The alternative was a hanging, so John of Ditchford abjured the realm. The port of Dover was assigned to him. He was required to give up all his possessions. A sword, a knife and clothing were taken from him, valued at 18 pence. He was given sackcloth to wear, and a small wooden cross to hold. He was told to walk directly to Dover. If he left the King's highway, he could be arrested. At Dover he would stand knee-deep in the sea until the next ship was leaving. He had to be on it. If he carried out all those instructions, he was safe from punishment for his confessed crime of murder.

All this must have been frustrating for Henry Felip's son, and those who sympathised with him. Robbery with violence, on the roads around, Northampton, was not a rare occurrence. The five robbers who had been captured would surely be hanged. It seemed a pity that this one should get away with it.

Clutching his little cross, John of Ditchford set off southwards, wearing his sackcloth robe. Two days later, he was found dead, minus his head, in the fields of Collingtree.

He had travelled less than a mile.

Richard Luvell, Coroner, now had a different task. He presided over an inquest into the cause of death of John of Ditchford.

The jurymen came from Wootton, Collingtree, Courteenhall and Rothersthorpe. They heard evidence that the deceased man had set off along the highway, heading for the assigned seaport of Dover. Near Collingtree, he suddenly left the King's highway and ran towards the woods. Spectators following at a distance had raised the hue and cry, so there was a chase. His head was cut off while he was trying to escape. He was in breach of sanctuary. No evidence was heard that Henry Felip's son had been involved.

The Coroner ordered the jurymen to carry the dead man's head to the King's Castle at Northampton.

Exactly ten years later, the Sheriff ordered an election for a new Coroner to replace Richard Luvell, because his qualifications were insufficient.

Northamptonshire Murder Tales, *Eric Jenkins, Cordelia, 1998, p 70, 71.*

He Played the Game

Lieutant Colonel Edgar Mobbs was a renowned rugby player who captained the Northampton Saints and England before the First World War, when he formed one of Kitchener's battalions. His friendly and warm personality compelled men to follow him and he won the DSO. He led from the front and his last encounter with the enemy was to charge, as in his wing three-quarter days, a well-sited machine gun post . . . he went down, leading the 7th (Service) Battalion, The Northamptonshire Regiment. His memorial stands in Abington Square, Northampton, and each year there is held a memorial rugby match.

A finer specimen of an English gentleman or a more thorough sportsman never existed. We all knew his sterling qualities on the football field, and never were they seen to better advantage than in the Army. A born leader of men, Lieut Colonel Mobbs never spared himself. I have seen him in the trenches at all hours of the day and night, often wet to the skin and covered in mud, but always cheerful with a word of encouragement for everyone, and he would visit dangerous points of the line whilst hesitating to send a subordinate.

His one thought was the welfare of those under him, and without exception he was loved by all. No one but we that joined with him in 1914 knew what he did for us, continually getting us out of little scrapes, begging for extra leave, and a hundred other things during our period of training in England, and helping us in every possible way when the real thing commenced.

Like all brave men, he never advertised himself, never sought popularity, there was no need. His personality and example were sufficient.

He had a hatred of red tape, and I remember an incident whilst we were in the trenches at St. Eloi, over our knees in mud and water, in October 1915. Some officious indispensable in England returned a form stating that certain portions should be filled up with red ink. Captain Mobbs (as he was then) sent it back stating that red ink was scarce in the trenches, but that he could find plenty of blood, if that would do!

I do not think that any name is better known or more widely respected in the Army today, than that of our late Colonel. I have hardly found anyone, Canadians, Anzacs, South Africans or British troops who did not know him, nor did I hear anything but praise.

We not only loved him, we looked up to him and boasted of him. We felt proud to belong to the Mobbs Regiment.

He had gone, having given his life in the greatest of all causes, his country's sake, but so long as that magnificent spirit of Bntish sportsmanship and fair play exists among us, so shall the name of Lieut Colonel Mobbs never be forgotten by us or by our comrades from overseas.

I know of no finer epitaph than: 'He played the game'.

God rest his soul.

The Mobbs Own, D. Woodall, Northamptonshire Regiment Association, 2000.

With God on our Side and a few Crumbs of Green Cheese

Early in the 17th century King James I began selling off Crown property, usually to the squires, but this was not without problems as local peasants suddenly found their settlements taken away from them. New hedges and fences were built, causing dismay and panic as their homes and livelihoods disappeared. Time for action, as the peasants, now known as 'The Levellers', lead locally by Captain Pouch, ripped down the hedges and fences.

The army of giant diggers worked swiftly, uprooting hedgerows, smashing fences, filling ditches.

Within hours the patchwork of tiny fields was transformed into a vast prairie, awaiting the plough, the seed drill and combine harvester. What John Reynolds would have given for a J.C.B. or two instead of an axe, a spade and a certainty that right was on his side.

But that was almost four hundred years ago. In 1607 to be precise. Hard up King James I had hit upon a novel idea for raising money to replenish his dwindling royal purse. He sold off Crown property, including acres of Royal Forest, to local landowners who clamoured to buy.

Squire Tresham purchased woodland around the village of Newton-in-the-Willows in Northamptonshire and proceeded to fell valuable timber, clear the ground and enclose the land as pasture for sheep. There was money in wool.

But he soon discovered problems lurking in the undergrowth. For centuries peasants had settled in the forests and on wasteland, building houses, raising families, cultivating the soil and making use of the plentiful fuel. They weren't vagrants or vagabonds but law abiding people, who over the years had come to regard this common land as their own.

Now they were confronted with hedges and fences where none had stood within memory, found roads and paths blocked as Tresham's estate grew and were turned out of their houses at the stroke of a lawyer's pen. Not surprisingly they didn't take kindly to the Squire's plans.

Faced with a choice either to abandon their homes and livelihoods and move away destitute, or to destroy the hedges and fences and stay put, they chose the latter.

They called themselves 'levellers' and rallied around their chosen leader. That man was John Reynolds.

Not a very heroic name was it? Hardly a Sir Francis Drake or Sir Walter Raleigh. John Reynolds didn't think so either. That's why he called himself Captain Pouch.

It was a strange but clever choice of name.

His followers had adopted the cause with good reason. Many were filled with a sense of injustice at being hustled from their homes and land. Others hated the landowners and welcomed a chance to get even. There was widespread support, even from the clergy. Parsons preached in local churches of the suffering, and hardship brought by enclosure upon displaced families, who were rather like modern day refugees. But this was also an age of superstition.

Reynolds announced that the great leather pouch hanging from his belt contained 'sufficient matter to defend against all corners'. In other words he claimed to possess a magic charm that would protect everyone who followed him, provided they, 'refrained from evil deeds'.

He also affected authority from both God and the King to 'throw down enclosures'.

All around the district as fast as fences were put up the levellers tore them down. But matters quickly came to a head when reports of rebellion reached London and the King.

A Royal Proclamation of May 30th 1607 instructed the Lord Lieutenant of the County, Sir Robert Cecil, and his deputies to 'immediately suppress (the levellers) by whatever means they may, be it force of arms if other lawful means do not serve and reduce them to their duties.'

It was the practice in such circumstances to call up the Trained Bands, a kind of Home Guard led by the local gentry, which each parish had to arm. In this instance, however, such a force could prove unreliable. Would they attack their own neighbours? Many sympathised with the levellers while others were actually related to members of Pouch's 'army'.

In the event the Lieutenants mobilised every reliable servant that local gentlemen could arm.

On the morning of June 8th, the two groups faced each other across the valley of the River Ise below Newton village. On one side, according to eye witnesses, as many as a thousand men and women, armed with half pikes, staves, bows, axes and stones. On the other, footmen with muskets and calivers.

Magistrates read a Royal Proclamation ordering the crowd to disperse.

No-one moved.

The order was repeated.

Perhaps an odd one or two slipped away. Then the attack began. A volley of shots was fired into the Tassed ranks.

Then charging horsemen drove deep into the crowd, scattering the levellers in all directions. They quickly regrouped but a second charge ended the battle. Captain Pouch's army was defeated.

Later the Earl of Shrewsbury wrote 'The first charge they stood and fought desperately: But at the second charge they ran away in which were slain some forty or fifty of them and a great number hurt'.

The dead and dying were carried to St Faith's church nearby. Punishment was swift and severe. Ringleaders were tried and executed, and their remains displayed around the County as a warning to others. Whether Captain Pouch died in the fight or was hanged after it is not certain. No records of the Assize Rolls or those killed in battle survive. But it is said that afterwards his famous pouch was opened and was found to contain. . . a few crumbs of green cheese.

What of the levellers who fought and lived?

The names of 143 are recorded in a document still extant, were required to sign a declaration promising to behave themselves for the rest of their lives:

'We and everyone of us whose names are here underwritten . . . do most humbly acknowledge our heinous offence . . . in the late rebellion . . . upon pretence of depopulation and unlawful inclosure and are most heartily sorry for the same. We acknowledge with all thankfulness his Majesty's gracious and exceeding clemency in setting wide open to us the gate of his mercy . . .

Occupations are listed too. They include butchers, bakers, labourers, shepherds, carpenters, coopers. Ancestors of local people almost certainly unaware of their rebellious forebears.

Today, Squire Tresham's hedges and fences around Newton are levelled by machines as pastures once more give way to the plough. But stand quietly in the shelter of St Faith's church, and close your eyes.

Listen.

That distant murmur might be the diggers, or traffic on the new motorway far across the valley. Or it might even be the ghosts of Captain Pouch's army massing in the fields below.

Moments of the Rose, Ian Addis, Jema Publications, 1994, pages 1-6.

10 · THE WORK FOLK

Although Northamptonshire is best known for its leather trade and in particular shoemaking, there are rich anecdotes to tell of other industries, be they cottage or of a more commercial nature.

Strife in the Shoe Industry

In 1857-59 several shoe manufacturers in Northampton wanted to introduce closing machines for the stitching together of the component parts of the shoe-uppers. The manufacturing of shoes had always been done by hand in the home and many shoemakers feared that this would lead to unemployment. An appeal printed in the local paper makes interesting reading.

TO THE BOOT AND SHOEMAKERS OF NORTHAMPTON

We address you on a matter of the greatest concern to you and to us. You live by work. We want work done on fair terms and for fair wages. That being so, our object is to establish those proper and just relations which should exist between employers and employed.

We have built, at a great cost, extensive premises in which to carry on the manufacture of boots and shoes. They are arranged upon the best plan. The rooms are large, lofty, and well ventilated, and kept warmed at an uniform, moderate, and healthy heat by nearly two miles of hot water piping.

They will be opened in a few days for the reception of workpeople; and we hope to see them filled by hundreds of busy hands.

The engagements will be permanent for all those who are willing to do, each day, a good day's work, under the superintendance of our foreman. The work will all be peace work.

The attendance must, for your sakes as well as for ours, be regular. The hours fixed are – in summer, from 6 to 8, from 8 to 12, and from 1 to 6 o'clock; and, in winter, from 8 to 12, from 1 to 4, and from 4 to 8.

The wages will be the same as those paid by other houses, and may be received daily or weekly, as you please.

Those who desire to do so may take two half-holidays in each week, namely, from the dinner hours of Wednesday and Saturday.

We intend to employ machinery. We state that plainly, because we know that many of you have striven against the introduction of machines; but we submit to you, and we are glad to know that many of you are aware of the fact, that machinery must and will be employed, and that to struggle against it is to fight with science, and to attempt to put a stop to the progress of the human mind.

We intend to employ women and children on the premises. Some of you have objected to that being done; but it is obvious that those women who work at machinery must be employed upon the premises. For them, separate work-rooms, entrances, stair-cases and personal accommodation have been provided; and they will be superintended entirely by females.

But we do not stipulate that married women and mothers of families shall work upon the premises, for we know that the house requires the presence of the wife; and the wives of men working for us may take out work.

No objection will be made to parents bringing their own children as apprentices to themselves.

Four men will work at each table. The men at each three of the tables may elect from among themselves an overseer, who will see that the work is properly done, and will be paid by us for such extra service.

There will be upon the premises a grindery store. The articles will be purchased wholesale for ready money, and sold to our workmen at cost price.

We have heard of your objections to what is called 'the factory system'. We submit to you that the system we propose is not the 'factory system'. It is a carefully considered system of constant, orderly, regulated work, without any of the bad features which have made the factory system distasteful to you; for example:

> Married women may have work at home;
> Parents may bring their children as apprentices;
> Men and women will be kept separate;
> Workmen will be allowed to choose their own overseers;
> Subdivision of labour will not be attempted.

The advantages which will accrue to the work-people can, we think, hardly be overlooked by you.

Instead of your being obliged to work in the close, confined rooms of your cottages, you will labour in healthy, commodious and well-ventilated apartments.

Your houses, instead of being ill-regulated workshops in which domestic duties interfere with labour, will become homes in which comfort will be possible.

You will be enabled to eat, sleep, and sit at your firesides free from the smell of the materials of manufacture, which, in small and crowded dwellings, is unpleasant, and may be unwholesome.

In regular hours of orderly labour, free from domestic hindrances, you will be able to do more work and earn more money in less time than you can now.

Your children employed under a well-regulated system will acquire habits of industry and order, and become more valuable to you.

Regular half-holidays will afford you opportunities for amusement and recreation.

We submit these important changes to you in all frankness, and in the hope and belief that you will see their reasonableness and advantage. You must be aware that we cannot suffer our premises to remain empty, and that if we cannot get work-people belonging to the town, we must obtain them from other places; but we had much rather employ those among whom we live, with whom we wish to be on the best terms, and to whom we have addressed these explanations, in the firm conviction that the acceptance of our proposals will be mutually beneficial, and that we shall have been privileged to conduce in no slight degree, towards the social, moral, physical and economical advancement of the honest and industrious artisans of the Borough of Northampton.

Northampton Mercury, 28 May 1859.

Outwork

The shoe industry was at its peak for about a hundred years between 1850 and 1950 but even when factory work became common-place, much work was still undertaken as 'outwork'. I have included a selection of interviews with shoe workers to give a flavour of the industry in its heyday.

'. . .as they issued the work you see, they gave you a work ticket with all the measurements and everything that had got to be done to the shoes; and I used to have to count all the stuff that went into the boots and shoes because, if I was anything short when I got home, my father had got to buy it himself. . .'
(Mr Joseph Marlow NBC T1/5)

'Grandmother, I've seen her sewing welts in and seen her making the thread and sew welt in the shoes and Uncle George's wife, the one who did the samples for Manfield's, I've also seen his wife sewing the welts in by hand and that was the way of life at that time . . .'
(Mr Joe Ellis b.1898 NBC T3/36)

'. . . they would only leave off to have their meals and they'd be working until nine, ten o'clock at night, and my mother, she used to stitch the shoes you see, because they were all welted the shoes were, and then my father would stitch the welts in and then when he got up to, he got the soles on and like that, my mother would stitch all round there by hand you see and she only used to get 9d (4fip) a pair . . . sometimes they wouldn't issue the flax to make them, to do it with, you'd have to buy your own flax. My father worked at home and as I say but unluckily for us my mother died just before the war finished, he couldn't work without my mother to do that stitching for him you see. Other than that he'd got to get another woman in the neighbourhood that did it to do it for him, but that wasn't always convenient, if they were working with their own husbands you see . .'
(Mr Joseph Marlow NBC T1/5)

'. . . they used to make most of their tools. My father made one, a buffing-knife, out of a motorbike nameplate, number-plate, and then there was when they used to start. They used to wet the leather so that it was nice and supple as they called it, they'd put it in the old tub and wet it and then they'd fetch it out and stand it up to drain and dry well and then they would hammer it all, nearly all the leather was hammered, and then they'd start by putting the toe bit, side-linings and stiffeners in the upper and trimming the insole to fit the last and then round the insole off, then they'd set a bit. Then they'd start by putting the upper onto the last with the insole on, they'd tack all of that round, they used to put that on with inch heel pins, but they always had the nails in their mouth, in their lip, so as they didn't have to keep putting their hand down to pick them up. There didn't have to be a crease or anything, they had to fit perfectly, then they would, when they'd lasted it they'd sew the seat in, that's round the heel, then they'd pick up the welt and go round with the welts and sew that in. Then when they'd done that they used to trim it and push the welt down so as it was nice and flat and then they used to put felting in, they heated it over a candle or little gas light so as it was nice and supple and then they'd heat the knife and then they'd trim that so that it filled up between the last and the welt because if you had two pieces of leather going together you would get a squeak and that was bad.'
(Miss Gwen Townsend NBC T1/13)

'. . . when he worked at home the people that I used to help fetch work from was from Green's factory at the top of Oliver Street and I used to have to fetch this work, take it home, then he used to do it you see and then take it back and fetch another load. That was his bread and butter work for a long time. . .'
(Mrs Flo Williams NBC T3/35)

'She (Mrs Roberts) lived at No. 75 Oliver Street and she made her, it was her house but she made her front room into a workroom and she had one, two, three machines in there, closing machines and so that would be two ladies working for her, and one used to take some work home from her and she used to do closing.'
(Mrs Flo Williams NBC T3/35)

'. . . the real workshops started with Lewis. It was a smaller place then, different altogether to today in that road when they went into the factories, but people used to work in their home. My father had a room as a factory and you'd fetch, well mother did, she fetched the parts and then he'd make them, then she'd take them back, book them in and pay him for what he'd done. They used to book it in them days what they'd done and you'd take this book to the main factory and they'd pay you at the end of the week according to what you'd got written down . . .'

(Mr Herbert Harrison b.1887 NBC T1/6)

'There was women fetched some of the shoes away and stitched them, stitched them round the welts see . . . Some of the men fetched the shoes out, all the bits, uppers, soles, heels and like that and it was my job at the start, getting all these bits together for these people coming in to fetch the shoes away . . . they used to come from Long Buckby and Cogenhoe and all over to fetch the shoes, but the best makers were at Cogenhoe and Long Buckby, some of our best makers made a pair of shoes right through and brought them back finished. We had a foreman who took, when they brought them back finished he looked at them up and down and passed them.'

(Mr Percy Goodman b.1897 NBC T1/14)

One lady outworker painted this picture of a young couple's lifestyle during the years between the two wars:

'You see before the war when we was young . . . nearly every house had a cellar with a bench and every man in the household could repair shoes because that was the in thing in Northampton, it was the shoe industry . . . they used to deliver, I think it was every day, round about lunch-time they used to bring me a big box of all the pieces of the shoes that needed . . . and they used to supply the cotton . . . and everything and I used to do as much as I can and the next day they'd collect and deliver . . . you'd get paid so much per dozen . . . and included in that price for the outdoor was your electricity you was using . . . they always used to send you the work that them indoors didn't like to do . . . early in the morning when my husband had gone to work (in a shoe factory) I thought right I'll give an hour, then I used to go up and do an hour or perhaps two then I used to come down and

get the lunch and the dinner and then in the afternoon I used to take
my boy out and then I'd be up there nearly all evening until it was time
for him to go to bed and if there was any work that needed sorting out
or colouring out I used to do that when he'd gone to bed . . .'
(*Anonymous Outworker b.1923 NBC T1/19*)

Stolen by the Gypsies

*Shoemakers always attended Boughton Fair, held towards the end of
June, and were often heard to recite 'The Ballad of Boughton Fair'.
Crispin, mentioned towards the end of the ballad, is the Patron Saint
of Shoemakers.*

With his beard in his bib the stichman wrought,
With his lapstone, leather and awl.
But he sometimes brushed from his clouded face
A tear for tears would fall.

And his hair on his drooping shoulders curled,
And his band round his brow was tied
And he said, "Tis the eve of Boughton Fair"
And he stitched and stitched and sighed.

Then he said "Come in" to a tap. She came.
And her eyes they were borage-blue.
And her hair like gold in the sunshine shone.
"I have scoured, Sir, the whole town through.

So you'll measure me, please, for shoes-and-shoes
That will wear for years and years,
And you'll make me a pair that shall fit me well,
Of leather and thread and tears."

"It is cruel to scoff the stitchman said,
At sorrow that no one can allay,
But inform me, who, for the wonderful shoes,
Will, when I have made them, pay."

If it's pay you want, no pay you'll have,
Yet you'll make, all the same, for me

The finest pair that you ever have made,
For I read folk's thoughts said she.

"It was at the Boughton Fair, ten years ago,
That you lost what you prized the most."
And the stitchman's face turned white as death
Or the face of a sheeted ghost.

"And what did I lose?" he trembling said,
"Why, you lost me, father, there,
For I am the girl whom the gypsies stole
From the stall at Boughton Fair."

And she flew to his arms and stopped his words
With Kisses .... at last he said
"I shall make them of tears, but they're bound to be tears
Of joy, and leather and thread."

... *and the ballad continues* ...

And they raised a cup to Crispin old,
And a cup to Crispin heir,
And a cup to the girl whom the gypsies stole
From the stall at Boughton Fair.

And at dawn the happy stitchman wrought,
As he'd wrought all the ten black years,
And the shoes were made of leather and thread
Of leather and thread and tears.

Taken from 'The Ballad of Boughton Fair', Manfield Magazine, No 1, 1929-30.

The Man in the Red Tie

Which general led an army 115 strong, on a route march 70 miles long to do battle with the Secretary of State for War? The answer, James Gribble, begs even more questions. It's a fascinating story.

There has been a centuries old tradition of boot and shoe making in Northamptonshire, due in part to the abundance of good grazing land for cattle and the profusion of oak forests providing bark for tanning. The industry had its humble origins in barns and sheds at the bottom of gardens, where whole families were engaged in the manufacture of the complete boot or shoe. By the 1850's it had developed into a primitive factory system like William Nichols' Grove Street establishment in Raunds. Here the clickers, (men who cut the leather according to patterns), were kept on the premises, but the closing, (hand sewing of the uppers), and making, (attaching the soles and heels), were put to outworkers. At this time shoeworkers prided their independence and were to some extent a law unto themselves. In his autobiography *The Vanished World,* H E Bates describes their inclination to '. . . get rousing drunk on Saturdays and Sundays, never by tradition working on Mondays. Either out of duty to their patron saint St Crispin or in pursuit of a cure for mountainous hangovers, they sought solace in the surrounding countryside . . .'

Such anarchic behaviour had no place in the regulated factory regimes which were becoming more widespread amongst the shoeworking communities. As the manufacturers began to enforce strict rules governing working hours, attendance and rates of pay, workers realised the need to protect their own interests. A first Trade union, the Amalgamated Cordwainers Association, became the National Union of Boot and Shoe Riveters and Finishers in 1874, and in turn the National Union of Boot and Shoe Operatives sixteen years later.

The industry was entering a critical period.

The Boer War had stimulated the need for army boots and for its duration, ensured relative prosperity for workers in the principal county centres of Raunds, Finedon, Irthlingborough, Higham Ferrers, Rushden, Wellingborough and Kettering. The end of hostilities however brought a slump with the immediate fall in demand. Factories began undercutting each other to get contracts and such contracts as were available were less lucrative than before. Not only was the rate paid to a skilled, proficient bootmaker reduced from a wartime peak of 3/11d (20p) per pair to 2/6d (12p) by 1905, but improved standards were imposed following claims that poor quality boots had been issued during the conflict.

Living standards fell as, "the average (worker) can do only six pairs in a 54 hour week."

Unemployment and short time working became commonplace. The small town of Raunds was particularly hard hit by the recession as during the war it had become the centre of Government contract work with a dozen boot factories employing over 1200 workers.

In the autumn of 1904 the Secretary of State for War, Mr Forster, was petitioned to implement a 'fair wages' clause in Government contracts in a bid to restore wage levels. He refused, but urged the men to use the power of their union to argue the case directly with manufacturers. The response of the National Union of Boot and Shoe Operatives was immediate and dramatic. Enter a short, stocky man wearing his habitual red tie.

James Gribble.

He was born at 25 Bailiff Street, Northampton in January 1868 the eldest child of a family of nine. His father, also James, worked in the shoe trade but was once landlord of the 'Marquis of Carabas' public house in Bouverie Street. Young James had only a rudimentary formal education at Spring Lane and Vernon Terrace Board Schools, before briefly attending the Northampton Evening School in his teens, for at' the age of 12 he had begun work for boot manufacturers Turner Brothers, Hyde and Co. Five years later in 1885 and unemployed, he enlisted in the regular army serving for eighteen months in England before moving overseas. He attained the rank of acting quarter master sergeant before demobilisation in January 1893.

On his return to civilian life and work in the boot trade, Gribble quickly became immersed in local union affairs. Despite a justifiable reputation for hotheaded unruly behaviour, which probably destroyed his chances of achieving high office in the Socialist movement, by Autumn 1904 he had been appointed National Union organiser and was sent to Raunds to stimulate activity at which point he takes centre stage in our story.

On March 11th 1905, having failed to achieve agreement with any local manufacturers to accept the uniform wage rates endorsed by the War Office, the Raunds bootmakers went on strike. In a speech typically radical and antagonistic towards these recalcitrant employers, Gribble described the town as, "a few compounds dumped there, surrounded by houses inhabited by white slaves, who ground out profits for the owners of the compound."

Although some manufacturers succumbed to Gribble's robust negotiating abilities, the hard core majority resisted. The strike dragged on into April leading to ugly scenes as the frustration of the workers spilled into violence, much of it directed towards the employers and strike breakers. The media had a field day.

Newspapers carried reports of riots, serious disturbances and extensive damage. The Manchester Guardian attempted to redress the balance reducing the 'riots' to 'accidental outbursts of horseplay', 'extensive damage' to 'window smashing' and dismissing the possibility of 'calling in the military' as 'irresponsible nonsense.'

With increasingly bad publicity generated by these disturbances, negotiations dead-locked, and a drift back to work by demoralised strikers, Gribble realised a dramatic gesture was required to regain public support. He decided to organise a march to London to put the strikers' case in person at the War Office. If the deputation was refused an audience it would march on to see King Edward VII at Windsor Castle.

There was no shortage of volunteers. Eventually 115 representative strikers were selected by 'General' Gribble who used his service experience to good effect. He was determined that the marchers would conduct themselves with dignity and discipline. The venture was planned with military precision. A Paymaster, Billetmaster and Commissariat-General were appointed as officers. Five companies were formed each with their own sergeants. The chosen men were drilled to perfection on a piece of wasteland near the Woodbine Club.

Monday, May 8th dawned clear and bright and the marchers set off from Raunds reaching Bedford that night.

Eleven bandsmen amongst the strikers borrowed instruments thus providing jaunty tunes to lead the marchers and raise the spirits. A corps of three cyclists rode ahead of the whole contingent. One unofficial marcher, Jack Pearson of Ringstead, went the whole distance on crutches!

After a public meeting on the Market Square at Bedford, accommodation was found in local homes, hotels and public buildings. The pattern was continued at Luton, St Albans and Watford before London was reached on Friday, May 12th.

Not one report in contemporary newspapers mentions hostility towards the marchers and everywhere contributions flooded into their strike collection fund. Ten thousand people gathered at Marble Arch to watch them arrive in the West End. Yet War Office officials at the Houses of Parliament refused to meet the deputation. Gribble, as ever resplendent in red tie, watched proceedings from the Strangers' Gallery becoming more and more annoyed by the likelihood that the strikers' case would never be heard. Characteristically his frustration boiled over.

He finally leapt to his feet and shouted, "Mr Speaker, is this gentleman trying to talk out time? For I've come here with 115 men from Northamptonshire who have marched all that way to lay their grievance before Mr Forster".

He was forcibly ejected. But not before it had been announced that an enquiry would be held in order to investigate wage levels in the army boot sector of the industry.

On Saturday evening James Gribble was part of an invited theatre audience who gathered to watch cinematographic film of the march. After the show, pride of place was reserved for Jack Pearson who demonstrated his expertise on crutches by bounding several times across the stage to rapturous applause.

The following afternoon 'The General' addressed a vast crowd in Trafalgar Square sharing the platform with numerous eminent speakers including Suffragette Leader, Mrs Despard and Keir Hardie, the founder of the Labour Party.

The return march was completed on Saturday, May 20th when Gribble was carried shoulder high into the Woodbine Club by an excited crowd. He had certainly put the little Northamptonshire town on the map. The War Office enquiry supported the strikers demands and a Board of Conciliation and Arbitration was set up to deal with future difficulties. Raund's position as a leading producer of Army and Navy boots was assured for years to come.

Although committed to the need to politically educate working people James Gribble never achieved his ambition to represent Northampton as a Social Democrat (then an extreme left wing socialist party), Member of Parliament, failing to be elected in both 1906 and 1910.

Ill health forced his gradual withdrawal from public life and in 1925 he retired to Hastings to take over the licence of a hotel there. Two years later he returned to Northampton, where he assisted in his wife's millinery business for several years. He died of a cerebral haemorrhage in Northampton General Hospital on August 14th 1934, aged 66 years old. Perhaps it is as well that he didn't live to witness the postwar decline in Northamptonshire's boot and shoe trade and the demise of the work force that he, 'General' Gribble had fought so hard to protect.

Moments of the Rose, *Ian Addis, Jema Publications, 1994, p 7-14.*

Does it Pay to Tell the Truth?

The Wesleyan Chapel in Syresham has an unusual memorial – John Kurde suffered for his religious beliefs after first being flung into one of the dungeons of Northampton Castle.

In memory of John Kurde, shoemaker, the Syresham martyr, burnt at the stake in defence of the truth, 1557. Tell ye your children of it, and let your children tell their children, and their children another generation.

Patron Saint of Spinning and Lace Making

St Catherine's Day, 25th November, was often observed as a holiday and celebrated with traditional food, drink and the singing of the rhyme.

> Here comes Queen Catherine, as fine as any Queen,
> With a coach and six horses a-coming to be seen;
> And a-spinning we will go, will go, will go,
> And a-spinning we will go.

> Some say she is alive, and some say she is dead,
> And now she does appear with a crown upon her head;
> And a-spinning we will go, will go, will go,
> And a spinning we will go.

> Old Madam Marshall she takes up her pen,
> And then she sits, and calls for all her royal men.

> All you that want employment, though spinning is but small,
> Come list and don't stand still, but go and work for all.

> If we set a-spinning, we will either work or play,

But if we set a-spinning we can earn a crown a day.

And if there be some young men, as I suppose there's some,
We'll hardly let them stand alone upon the cold stone.
And a-spinning we will go, will go, will go,
And a-spinning we will go.

Wanted Able Bodied Men and Young Boys and Girls

*But not paupers who settled in Weedon! As a liability on the Parish
they would be removed by the Parish Officers but an Act of 1762,
passed after the Seven Years War, allowed discharged militia to obtain
regular employment without them being removed.*

WEEDON, DECEMBER 20TH 1768.

This is to give NOTICE,

To all Parishes which have got poor Boys and Girls, about thirteen
or fourteen years of age, and want to ease their Parishes.

That there is now an opportunity of setting them, as yearly
Servants, to the SILK MANUFACTORY at Weedon, Northamptonshire, to
the amount of fourscore or an hundred. Likewise are wanted, at the
same place, ten or twelve men, such as have served the King, either as
Soldiers or Sailors, it matters not how large their families are, as none
will be accepted, but such as the Parish-Officers cannot remove,
meaning the men and their families. Let those apply to the place above
mentioned.

Northampton Mercury, *26th December 1768.*

But not all were Honest

SATURDAY, MARCH 28TH, 1772.

Whereas James England, of Weedon-Beck, in the County of
Northampton, Ribbon-Weaver, who stands charged with stealing
Silks to the Amount of One Thousand pounds and upwards, and with
many other atrocious Felonies, made his Escape early this Morning
from a Constable at the Saracen's Head at Daventry, in the same
County. Any Person who will give information of him to Mr. Robert

Clarke, at the Saracen's Head aforesaid, or to Sir John Fielding, Knt. or to David Wilmot Esq., or any other of his Majesty's Justices of the Peace for the County of Middlesex, so that he may be retaken, shall receive TEN GUINEAS over and above the Reward allowed on Conviction by Act of Parliament. And any Person who will discover where the said Silks are so that they may be recovered, shall receive a proper and adequate Reward for his Trouble. The said James England is about forty-seven years of age, five Feet five or six Inches high, has full hazel Eyes, thick-set and square, has a Sea-faring and Weather-beaten appearance, has many Wounds upon his Head and in different Parts of his Body, wears a Wig, and the general Turn of his Conversation is directed to Travelling, Voyages, Mechanics, and discovering Mines, and the North-West Passage, and he has declared (for some Time past) an Intention of going to North-America.

Northampton Mercury, *April 6th 1772.*

Lace for Royalty

Her most gracious Majesty the Queen has been pleased to honour Mr Rose, Lacemaker and gold blonde worker of Paulerspury, Northamptonshire, with an order for a white lace scarf, veil and setter to be made of Paulerspury lace.

Northamptonshire Mercury and Northampton Herald, *June 16th 1847.*

Phipps Breweries

Phipps Breweries probably came to Northampton when a purpose-built brewery became available and was leased from John Barratt in 1817.

WHARF BREWHOUSE, ETC, NORTHAMPTON TO LET

JC Barratt respectfully informs his friends and the public that in consequence of Messrs Wilson, Hanson and Fascutt declining the further wish of establishing a public ale and porter brewery in Northampton, as intended and agreed, on the premises of JC Barratt in Bridge Street adjoining the River Nene or Nen and communicating with the Grand Junction Canal, JC Barratt finds his present business, independent of the above mentioned brewery falling on his hands, more than he can manage with pleasure to himself and family, is determined on declining some part of his concerns, he therefore wishes to inform the public, that he intends letting his present business at Northampton, with the addition of a large commodious house fit for the reception of a family of the first respectability together with a new and complete dwelling house and offices in the occupation of Mr C Duke, his bookkeeper, divided from the above only by a gateway or entrance to the said wharf and premises. The outer offices consist of a newly erected and very complete brewery, cellars, storerooms etc; large maltings and malt chambers, extensive warehouses capable of containing several thousand quarters of grain, a stable etc. The advantage for establishing a brewery viz convenience of land and water carriage, one of the best barley markets, coals cheap, no brewery in the place, a large and populous town and neighbourhood and within a short distance two sets of Barracks and deposits for Government stores. For further particulars to JC Barratt, Woodford Lodge near Thrapston. The brew house is provided with a plant calculated to be complete as any house now in use, the copper set and finished by the first workmen, and the remainder of the utensils ready for fixing up and may be taken at valuation.

Northampton Mercury, *18th January 1817.*

Hard Times for the Entrepreneur

Bankruptcy caused the sale of Thomas Grose's brewing business.

Lot 2, comprises of an important business, consisting of a wholesale and retail brewery, in full trade. The brewery buildings are substantially erected, and are capable of brewing 70 barrels per week, with a copper furnace containing 375 gallons, a 6 quarter mash vat, underback, three large coolers and a large square working tun, containing 22 barrels, the whole nearly new; 2 large casks containing 1,200 gallons each; and other casks of different sizes, containing 2,600 gallons and upward, one underground cellar, capable of holding 4,000 gallons, and two other cellars capable of holding 1,500 gallons, the whole well supplied with good water from two pumps, together with a new built brick and slate messuage or dwelling house adjoining the said brewery stabling for five horses. The whole calculated for an extensive and good business, which has been carried on upon the said premises for many years by Mr Thomas Grose.

Northampton Mercury, *17th July 1830.*

Welton's Smithy

There was a blacksmith at Welton, Mr Harrison, whose forge was under the horse chestnut tree next to the dairy. I can remember the smell of the hot metal now and the sound of the hammer, mixed up with the sweet milky smell of the cow's breath as they were driven up the street twice a day to be milked, and my mother's grumbling at the cow pats they dropped.

Northamptonshire Within Living Memory, *Northamptonshire Federation of Women's Institutes, Countryside Books, 1992, p 43.*

Northamptonshire Seed Cake

A plain cake flavoured with nutmeg and caraway seeds, traditionally served at sheep shearing time.

8 oz butter, 8 oz flour, 8 oz caster sugar, ½ teaspoon baking powder, 4 eggs, 1 teaspoon ground nutmeg, 1 oz caraway seeds.

Set oven to 350°F or Mark 4. Grease and line an 8 inch round cake tin. Cream the butter and sugar together in a bowl until light and fluffy. Place the eggs in a bowl set over a saucepan of hot water and whisk until fluffy, then whisk into the butter mixture. Sift the flour and baking powder together and fold into the mixture, together with the nutmeg. Add the caraway seeds and combine well. Turn into the prepared tin and smooth over the top. Bake for 1fi-2 hours, covering the top with a piece of kitchen foil if it appears to be browning too quickly. Cool in the tin for 5 minutes, then turn out on to a wire rack.

English Teatime Recipes, *Salmon, p 13.*

11 · CHALK AND TALK

Life's Rich Pageant

Oundle Public School had a succession of strong headmasters, none more so than Dr Fisher (Headmaster 1922-45), who upheld Victorian traditions.

As in other public schools, Victorian ethics still prevailed, and Fry's legacy lingered on in the shape of strict regulations governing conduct: roll-calls were taken at least twice a day; there were bounds beyond which none but prefects might go; no fraternising was allowed between boys of different houses. The uniform dress was grey flannel suits with waistcoats, stiff collars (Eton collars for new boys) and black ties, or black coats with striped trousers on Sundays. Crested black caps were worn in the winter, straw 'bashers' in the summer term. The tone was oppressively evangelical: prayers before breakfast, prayers in the Great Hall before school, prayers in the evening; at least two chapel services on Sundays, plus holy communion for those who had been confirmed; scripture lessons after chapel; the usual complement of house prayers. Grace before every meal. And so on, and so on.

Daily life was regulated by bells – Betjeman's 'inexorable bells; to early school, to chapel, to school again: compulsory constipation, hurried meals.' The pressure to hurry everywhere, from classroom to classroom with armfuls of books; to change hastily and rush up to the field for games or OTC drill; to plunge in one's turn into hip baths full of hot muddy water left by the previous occupant, or cold hip baths for a mandatory twenty seconds before breakfast or early school; to hand one's exeat card to the housemaster within the required space of time when one had been to some extra, mural activity – the dread of being late was perpetually present. But all this was stoically accepted as an inherent part of school life. There was very little time for leisure in Fisher's Oundle, which meant that there was not much scope for mischief either. This was, of course, the underlying motive for keeping every moment of the day filled with some planned activity, so that a sort of amnesia was necessary to keep up with the stringent and single, minded routine. Covert longings there may have been, affaires de coeur undoubtedly occurred, but sensual lusts were effectively thwarted. There was, I would say, very little if any of the sexual horseplay which apparently disfigured school life elsewhere, and which Oundle boys simply regarded as 'smut'.

Oundle and the English Public School, *Raymond Flower, Stacey International 1989, p 114, 115.*

Please Sir, 'Can I have some more?'

On a personal note I find this extremely interesting and wonder whether the schoolmaster ever did have that status in society that he is proported to have had. John Graves was the first President of the National Union of Teachers!

HANGING HOUGHTON.

MARCH 19TH, 1859.

TO THE TRUSTEES OF LAMPORT CHARITY.

GENTLEMEN,

You are perhaps aware that for the last 9 months, in consequence of the breaking out of fever at Houghton, and other causes over which I had no control, the number of children attending my school has been greatly diminished, and this entirely from those coming from other parishes, and from whom I have been in receipt of payment. The number thus lost is about 12; and this loss of scholars has considerably reduced my income, so that I have now very little more than the regular endowment to support my family upon, which I find quite insufficient to maintain it as respectably as I ought: I am, therefore, impelled, though with great reluctance, to ask if an increase could not be made to my salary.

These are the points I would respectfully submit for your consideration:-

1. My income, in consequence of the circumstances above mentioned, is decreased on the average of the 5 years previous to June last, nearly £20 per annum.

2. The salary paid by the Trustees is, alone, insufficient to maintain any person with a family in that degree of respectability which his calling and station in life demand and which he is expected by all to keep up: for £30 - my own salary - about 11/6 per week, little if any more than the generality of farm labourers receive, and certainly not enough to do it. The £15 allowed for the mistress I have been unable to derive much benefit from, because of being necessitated to keep some one to attend to my family, who, perhaps, might have been dispensed with had our school not been detached from the house as formerly. I have, however, found it necessary to do this in order to properly discharge the duties of the situation.

3. While holding this situation, I am cut off from all professional advancement. This is because the school has an endowment for its maintenance. I cannot obtain from the Committee of Council, a Certificate of Merit, and without it, to say nothing of the pecuniary advantages accompanying it, it is almost useless to attempt to obtain a situation worth trying for. I have three times applied to be I allowed to sit for examination, but have been as many times refused permission to do so. Had I had this requisite I might at this moment have been in receipt of an income of £130 a year.

I hope Gentlemen, you will not think me impertinent in thus explicitly stating the above circumstances: but I felt it necessary to do so: I have now held this office 8 years, and I trust I have been able during that period to discharge my duties satisfactorily, as I can conscientiously say I have endeavoured to do. I have no desire to remove from my present situation, and were I to do so, it would be with great regret, experiencing as I have often done many kindnesses at your hands, and for which I should be very ungrateful were I ever to forget them; yet, and I have no doubt you will think with me, so long as I have others depending on me for support, it is a duty incumbent on me to endeavour to do my best to maintain them in that station in which our lot is cast.

In conclusion, allow me, Gentlemen, to ask you to take this application into your most favourable consideration.

I am, Gentlemen,

Your Obedient Servant,

John J. Graves.

Northamptonshire Past and Present, *Vol IV, No 1, 1966/67, p 9, 10.*

Doom'd to Teach, and Doom'd to Toil

Thomas Bell, living in Barnwell, writes with passion and feeling about his life as a schoolmaster and of his tough personal experiences during the early nineteenth century.

Who is he, pacing slowly
    Up and down the village green,
Folding arms, and thinking deeply,
    On a summer's eve is seen?
Winter's cold will find him seated,
    Musing by the glimm'ring light,
That, from half extinguish'd candle,
    Darker makes the gloom of night.
With broken heart, and aching head,
    Toiling for his daily bread.

Bright the sun shone on his childhood,
    On his manhood fortune smil'd;
Friends abounded, honours courted,
    While the muse his hopes beguil'd.
Ere his harvest had been gather'd,
    Storms arose to cloud the sky,
Leaving him with prospects blighted,
    Here to weep and here to die.
Truly has the poet shown,
    Hapless man was made to mourn.

Bent by age, by sorrows wasted,
    Worn his frame, and dim his eye;
Threadbare garments plainly showing
    What his frugal means supply.
Coarse his fare, and that but scanty;
    From his fate too proud to shrink,
Bread his food, with little added,
    Water from the spring his drink.
Hope extinguish'd in his breast,
    Longing for eternal rest.

Such the luckless lot of many,
    Doom'd to teach, and doom'd to toil;
Working harder, earlier, later,
    Than the clown, that tolls the soil.
'Tis not want that breaks the spirit;
    'Tis not toil that sinks the heart;
But, to find his name forgotten,
    Wings the shaft, and points the dart.
Is this true? the reader cries;
    Too true, alas! the muse replies

The Rural Album, *Thomas Bell, 1853.*

The Value Of Religious Instruction

SATURDAY 23 JANUARY 1904
FAWSLEY

Education Committee. Horrified at the proposal to deduct from the teachers' salaries the amount due for the 'time employed in religious instruction'. Very few of our people were there, so we were beat by 10 to 4. It don't really matter, as it is referred to the Board of Education, but it is the spirit, and still worse, on the proposal to provide Bibles for the schools, the co-opted Board School master strongly objected to the Bible in schools at all.

Politics and Society, The Journals of Lady Knightley, *P. Gordon, Northampton Record Society, 1999, p 366.*

12 · LEISURE

The Lords at Rowell Races

5 SEPTEMBER 1672

We went to Rowell (Rothwell) races, which are held in a suitable spot enclosed by hills, from which there is a view down on to a level stretch two miles long and four hundred yards wide. They go twice round this course before passing the post. Four horses ran; first Lord Exeter's, ridden by Lisle; the second Lord Cullen's, which he rode himself; the third Lord Brudenell's, ridden by Mr Washbourne, and the fourth Lord Sherard's, whose rider was Lord Westmorland. Thee prize was set (two silver candlesticks) and they mounted and waited the signal with tight rein; when the horn sounded its clarion note they leapt away from the starting-point and a great shouting rent the air. Cullen at first rode far ahead, next came Westmorland and third Lisle, and Washbourne followed Lisle. They headlong sieze the plain and lay on their blows, and at length Westmorland outstripped the rest and won the first race. The whole amphitheatre resounded with applause and the shouts of men. Meanwhile they rested their limbs and wiped the sweat from their horses. Mr Mulsoe of Finedon and Somers, Cullen's servant, have a dispute about the venison that Mr Mulsoe brought. When this race was run the jockeys dart forth again from the starting-point and strive for long, while the issue is in doubt, but on almost the last lap, as they were coming up to the post, Lisle went ahead to win. The last race now came, in which there were only three competitors, as Washbourne had retired in the previous race. They take their places, fired with love of glory, and suddenly dart over the plain at the given signal. Lisle rides ahead, mad with excitement, but when he was filled with hope of bearing off the palm, he rode down a man and, poor fellow fell from his horse! Then the two last, Westmorland and Cullen, were filled with joyous hope of passing the laggard Lisle; Westmorland takes first place and, fired by his own success, plies the cracking whip and passes the post first, flying 'mid the plaudits and cheering shouts of the mob – while the hills resound with the clamour. I rode the brown horse, and as soon as I came to the course a veterinary came up to me and offered me eighteen pounds for the animal; he approached my father with the offer, but father declined.

The Diary of Thomas Isham of Lamport 1671-73, *translated by N. Marlow.*

Oundle Town Races 1722

On Tuesday the 11th Day of September next, a Purse of 15l. Value will be Run for on Oundle Course in the County of Northampton, by any Horse, Mare or Gelding carrying 10 Stone weight, the best of 3 Heats: The winning Horse, &c. to be thrown for at 20l. by the Contributors there present. A Subscriber to pay 1 Guinea, and a Non-Subscriber two Guineas Entrance. The next Day a Purse of 10l. will be Run for on the same Course, by Galloways carrying 9 Stone weight the highest, to carry Weight for Inches, the Best of 3 Heats. A Contributor to pay Half a Guinea Entrance, if not a Contributor, a Guinea. And on Thursday 13th, the Gentlemens Contribution of 30 odd Guineas will be Run for on the same Course, by any Horse, & carrying 12 Stone weight, the best of 3 Heats. The winning Horse, &c. to be Sold for 40l. A Contributor to pay 1 Guinea, if not a Contributor, 2 Guineas Entrance. All the Horses, &c. that Run for any of these Purses, are to be shown and entered before the Clerk of the Race on the 4th of September next, at the Town Pump in the New Street, between the Hours of 1 and 8 in the Afternoon, and to stand at such Public Houses only in the said Town as contribute 1 Guinea or more to the Town Purses.

Note: There will be an Assembly all the time of the Race, and on Friday Morning a Cock-Match between 2 private Gentlemen, will be fought 20 Pair of Cocks 2 Guineas a Battle, and 10 Guineas the odd Battle. In the Afternoon wilt be a Foot Race for a Pair of Buck-Skin Breeches, Gentlemens Running Footmen excepted. And also a Saddle of 40s. Value to be Run for by any Horse, &c.

Stamford Mercury, *9 August 1722*.

A Perilous Balloon Ascent

Yesterday night, Mrs. Graham attempted to ascend from Northampton, with a balloon, which had been expanded for the purpose of taking up two persons, but in removing it from the gas works, after its inflation, to the Market-square, it was rent nearly a foot in length by coming in contact with some chimneys, which occasioned so great an escape of gas as to make it apparent that one person only could possibly ascend, – and Mrs. Graham was the adventurer. The vessel, however, had not sufficient buoyancy to take her safely over the house, and she was compelled to leave it, and with assistance to get into the widow Ager's attic window, amidst a volley of brickbats and mortar thrown down from a chimney which the balloon was all the while beating against.

After it was thus lightened, it arose over the houses, and going in a south-east direction, fell in the front of Mr. Croft's house, at Tansor, near Oundle. The car became detached and dropped into the river Nene, which was about to be dragged from a supposition that the aeronaut must be drowned, but the course of the balloon was followed by a person from Northampton, who explained the affair. These balloon ascents begin to lose their attraction, for we learn that the contributions on the present occasion did not amount to above one fourth of the expenses incurred.

Drakard's Stamford News, *31 October 1828*.

Chapel Curve

Motor-racing enthusiasts all over the world will be familiar with Chapel Curve which is part of the Silverstone motor racing circuit. Few of them know that there was a Methodist chapel and a group of cottages huddled together beside a copse in a tiny settlement called Chapel Green. A double-fronted house, Maggotts Moor Lodge, used as a gamekeeper's cottage, stood a little way off at the entrance to a riding into the Whittlebury Forest. Legend has it that a chapel dedicated to St Thomas a Becket, no longer visible, was built in earlier times, hence the name Chapel Copse. The Methodist chapel and the cottages on the green were all demolished in 1939, somewhat urgently, to make way for the building of a war-time airfield. After the war the Royal Automobile Club acquired the land with its runways to found the now famous Silverstone motor racing circuit, home of the British Grand Prix.

Northamptonshire Within Living Memory, *Northamptonshire Federation of Women's Institutes, Countryside Books, 1992, p 67.*

Cinema Pioneer

Oundle had the first municipal cinema in the country, which was opened in 1947 in the Victoria Hall and run by the council. The opening was announced on the radio in a programme called In Britain Now. The usherette was Miss Richards, a grey-haired lady, with a torch who would rush up and say, 'Are you boys behaving yourselves in the front there?'

There were three prices: 10d in the first three rows, 1s 9d in the middle and 2s 3d in the back three rows. There were three changes of film a week and two showings of each one. I think Alec Wright did some of the projection work.

Andrew Spurrell in Voices of the Nene Valley, *J. Spelman, Tempus Books, 2001, p 99.*

13 · STRANGE ENCOUNTERS

Bleak House

Charles Dickens was a frequent visitor to Rockingham Castle during the mid-nineteenth century, incorporating observations made whilst at the castle into Bleak House. *It is possible that the Ghost's Walk at Chesney Wold corresponds to the Yew Walk at Rockingham.*

The day waned into a gloomy evening, overcast and sad, and I still contended with the same distress. I went out alone, and, after walking a little in the park, watching the dark shades falling on the trees, and the fitful flight of the bats, which sometimes almost touched me, was attracted to the house for the first time. Perhaps I might not have gone near it, if I had been in a stronger frame of mind. As it was, I took the path that led close by it.

I did not dare to linger or to look up, but I passed before the terrace garden with its fragrant odours, and its broad walks, and its well-kept beds and smooth turf; and I saw how beautiful and grave it was, and how the old stone balustrades and parapets, and wide flights of shallow steps, were seamed by time and weather; and how the trained moss and ivy grew, about them, and around the old stone pedestal of the sun-dial; and I heard the fountain falling. Then the way went by long lines of dark windows, diversified by turreted towers, and porches, of eccentric shapes, where old stone lions and grotesque monsters bristled outside dens of shadow, and snarled at the evening gloom over the escutcheons they held in their grip. Thence the path wound underneath a gateway, and through a courtyard where the principal entrance was (I hurried quickly on), and by the stables where none but deep voices seemed to be, whether in the murmuring of the wind through the strong mass of ivy holding to a high red wall, or in the low complaining of the weathercock, or in the barking of the dogs, or in the slow striking of a clock. So, encountering presently a sweet smell of limes, whose rustling I could hear, I turned with the turning of the path, to the south front; and there, above me, were the balustrades of the Ghost's Walk, and one lighted window that might be my mother's.

The way was paved here, like the terrace overhead, and my footsteps from being noiseless made an echoing sound upon the flags. Stopping to look at nothing, but seeing all I did see as I went, I was passing quickly on, and in a few moments should have passed the lighted window, when my echoing footsteps brought it suddenly into my mind that there was a dreadful truth in the legend of the Ghost's Walk; that it was I, who was to bring calamity upon the stately house; and that my warning feet were haunting it even then. Seized with an augmented terror of myself which turned me cold, I ran from myself and everything, retraced the way by which I had come, and never paused until I had gained the lodge-gate, and the park lay sullen and black behind me.

Bleak House, *Charles Dickens, 1853*.

A Ghost in the Church

Small church is to close. There were a few paragraphs in the local paper, but it is the usual matter of accountancy, a congregation of nine unable to afford repair bills of £150,000. But this is no ordinary church – this is St Guthlac's at Passenham in Northamptonshire. Come inside for a moment.

It is a summer evening and there are shadows on the two inscriptions above the south door. Both are in Latin. The first celebrates the rebuilding of the chancel in 1626 and the text is what you would expect. Psalm 116, verse 12, 'How can I repay the Lord for his goodness to me?' But the second text is not at all what you would expect. St Luke 12, verse 20, *Stulte Hoc Nocte* . . . 'You fool, this very night your life will be demanded of you.'

The church guide-book, its words chosen with care, describes this as an enigma in its context. It does not mention the story, still told, that when the man who had the chancel rebuilt came to be buried, his bearers heard a known voice speak from the coffin. 'I am not ready.' They opened the coffin but there was no movement in the wild spade-bearded face, which now, in marble, is also in the chancel wall. Yet when they buried him beside the altar the voice spoke again, 'I am not ready yet.'

And you are in familiar territory, are you not? An English parish church; a puzzling quotation; a dominating long-dead local figure. All you are waiting for is the horror to come as quietly as the tide and break among stone flags, and the damp, for in life you have stepped into a ghost story by M.R. James.

Three-and-a-half centuries after his death they still remember Sir Robert Banastre in Passenham, mothers bringing children to order by the mention of his name. Architectural historians also remember him. His chancel, said one, was unique. And it is. Sit down, for the restoration work of the 1950s has restored it to the way it would have looked in Banastre's time. You will have already noticed that you are in an unusual place, entering from the west through the bell tower, past the eighteenth-century boxed pews painted a pale matt green.

And then you come to Banastre's chancel.

Even old Pevsner was startled into one of his rare, wintry adjectives. 'Very remarkable furnishings,' he wrote. The roof is a deep blue, sprinkled with gold stars so you feel you have strayed into a planetarium. But everything else is deliberately archaic. On the walls are paintings of biblical figures, not put up to overawe the poor, but huge and elegant. The only thing is, they were put up centuries after the fashion for wall paintings had gone, and just before it became imperative to whitewash them over. The man who had this done must have thought himself in his private chapel, and where St Mark should be, his own face, under a linen skullcap, looks down.

And Sir Robert had only just begun. His choir stalls froth with carvings and there are misericords from a time long after these had gone out of ritual. You sit there, passing your hands over carvings in the twilight, and you have the odd sensation these are moving. So you bend to look, and wish you hadn't. For these are not the quaint beasts of the Middle Ages, these were meant to terrify: hoofed demons, legs shaggy with hair, their mouths agape, eyes bulging, breasts sagging.

Why did he have all this done? It has been suggested Banastre was a secret Catholic, this prominent courtier to James I and Charles I, but no secret Catholic would have dared commission anything like this. And why did his villagers hate him so? The local historian Sir Gordon Roberts thought it might be because Banastre had enclosed their common land, but this, he found, had been done long before. As for the stories of cruelty, he found that Banastre's will bulged with bequests.

Yet they did hate him and went on hating him and told so many ghost stories these have become matter of fact. I asked one man when he had last seen a ghost, and he said Tuesday night, when a voice spoke out of the darkness. A human shape? Oh yes, except this was a human shape in a large hat with a feather.

How odd it should feel so remote here, for the main road is only half a mile away and over the water meadows the roofs of Milton Keynes show above the willow trees, massed like an army. There are just fifteen houses in Passenham, also a tithe barn, the manor, the church. And if it is remote now, think how much more it must have been in the early seventeenth century, when a powerful man might have done what he wanted here.

A summer evening with shadows, and the sudden wish to be elsewhere.

An Audience With An Elephant, *Byron Rogers, Aurum Press 2001, pages 258-260.*

The Legend of Stowe Nine Churches

The village of Church Stowe, often called Stowe Nine Churches is a small hamlet near Daventry and perches high on a hill with wide views over the rolling countryside. There is a charming legend, set in Anglo Saxon times, about the origin of its unusual name.

One day the Lord of Stowe was out riding when he came to a steep ridge where he could look down on the surrounding countryside. He reigned in his horse and surveyed the scene before him. His gaze took in the rich pastures and dense woods, he could also see the serfs toiling on the strips of ploughed land. The Thane was proud of the fact that this part of the country belonged to him and his family. He rode on and noticed that the serfs had finished their work for the day and had gathered round a monk, who was telling them a simple parable from the Bible.

His audience were tired and found it difficult to understand what the monk was saying. They had been working a long hard day and only wanted to get home to eat their meal and rest for the night. The holy man saw that they were inattentive, so he blessed them and sent them on their way.

The Thane guided his horse over to the monk and spoke to him. 'You are wasting your time, Father,' he said, 'they are very tired and only want warmth and shelter after a days toil, it is the wrong time to speak to them'.

The Holy man agreed with the Thane and said sadly that what they really needed was a church, where the people could sit.in comfort and listen to the word of God. He pointed to the castle at the top of the hill and said that the Thane had a fine home to shelter him and keep him warm, but all that his workers had was the open sky and cold wind.

The Thane of Stowe felt guilty and apologised to the monk for not helping him to build a church. 'Come with me to the castle', he said, 'and we can plan where to build a fine stone church'.

The Monk and the Thane went up the hill together and entered the castle where they sat by the blazing log fire and discussed ideas for the building. The monk said he would like the church to be built in the valley by the stream. For they would need water for the baptisms. The Nobleman agreed with him and said it would also be near the village and his people would not have far to walk to church. Then he willingly gave his permission for the work to start on clearing the ground on a level piece of land in the vale.

The next day the monk took the masons and the labourers down to the new site. The men began to dig the trenches for the foundations and in the evening they went home well satisfied with their day's labour.

On the next morning when they arrived on site, they were dismayed to see that the trenches had been filled again. But they set to work with determination and cleared the trenches out and started to lay the stones for the walls. Yet on the following day they went to work, not only were the ditches filled in with soil, but the stones were scattered about the valley. The monk stood by and watched the men restart the digging once more and was puzzled and angry as to why the new church should be vandalised.

The Master builder encouraged his labour force as best he could and the walls began to rise. They finished work for the night well pleased with their efforts. On the third morning they returned to find their work had been demolished overnight. This happened eight times and the builders became very resentful and despondent.

The monk said that one of them must keep watch for the night. No one wanted to stay behind for they were frightened. Then, one brave man volunteered and the monk came to see him after dark to make sure all was well.

At day break the workmen were on the site very early. The night watchman was safe and calm, but he had a strange tale to tell. All had gone well until midnight and then a dark shape had appeared over the brow of the hill. He couldn't see it very well as it was a moonless night, but he said, 'It was a crettur no bigger nor a hog'. It moved quickly and without any seeming effort the creature had picked up the stones and hurled them about the vale, then it had filled in the trenches with soil. It had only stopped work when the cock crowed and it had started to get light. Then the monster ran off over the hill.

The labourers were astonished to hear the news and they all began to speak at once. It was Beelzebub, it was the devil himself, but the commanding voice of the monk silenced them. He said it was nothing of the kind, but a messenger from God. It had been sent to make them understand that they had started to build the church in the wrong place.

'We must start again, but this time it must be high on a hill top where villagers from miles around will see the tower and hear the bell. Come follow me'. The holy man held up his cross and led the procession up the steep incline until they came to the top of the hill over looking Weedon. Then, for the ninth and last time they started to build their church. The men sang as they worked and the building progressed well. Nothing or no one hindered them and the Thane came to inspect the work and heartened them on.

When the strong but simple stone church had been completed, the monk and the villagers rejoiced as the bell rang out over the valley and that is how the village of Stowe Nine Churches got its strange name.

A more prosaic explanation is that the Lord of the Manor had the right of presentation to nine local churches in medieval times.

Whichever story you care to believe, the small church of St Michael's can still be seen to this day, with its fine Saxon tower overlooking the main street of Stowe.

Ghosts and Folklore of Northamptonshire *Vol 3, Marian Pipe, Spiegl Press 1986, pp 61-64.*

The Grey Lady

James Manfield, the son of Sir Phillip Manfield, inherited the family shoe business in 1889. A Jacobean style house in 100 acres of land was built for the family between 1899 and 1902. James' attempted to sell this in 1923 and 1924 but the house did not receive the reserve price. After an article in the Northampton Independent *newspaper he gave the house and 19 acres to the 'Crippled Children's Fund'. The house was opened as Manfield Orthopaedic Hospital on 26 February 1926. James' favourite saying was perhaps indicative of his sympathy and empathy for children needing help:*

'The way to have friends is to be one.'

Stories of the presence on the estate of a ghost known as The Grey Lady were not uncommon.

Was that a figure I saw floating by?
Or my senses playing a trick on my eye.
Did I see her pass close by the lake?
Or in the mist did I make a mistake.

A cold, clammy sweat passed over my brow
I had to go forward and find out now.
My heart pounded and my poor head ached,
My hands trembled and whole body quaked.

I could not think straight for fear and fright.
The mist swirled round as though it was night
And then I saw her again I was sure,
Was suddenly happy, serene, safe, secure.

The beautiful lady dressed in grey
Was urging me join her, join her and pray
For children with bodies, broken and bent
She said this place was from heaven sent.

To give them the chance to live once again
To run and play in the sun and the rain.
Once more she spoke and I knew it was true:
'The present day problems I leave to you,

Save the house' she said again and again
'So others, not children are freed from pain
With beauty of nature to show that life
Her purpose and meaning, is not just strife.'
Commemoration of Manfield, *Headway House Educational Group, July 1992.*

The Ghosts of Boughton Green

A profusion of ghost stories surround the deserted village at Boughton Green, just outside Northampton, where the derelict old church now stands, overgrown with trees, brambles and years of decay. Perhaps this story attempts to solve the ghostly affairs!

CHRISTMAS, 1708

Now I, John Wakefield, have thought it proper to set down these things that follow, for a lesson to those that come after, and for a serious warning. It hath for some time past, been the habit of this our parish of Kyngsthorpe, to give credit to an idle tale, that on the eve of Christmas a ghost may be seen in the old churchyard on Boughton or Buckton Greene, near by our parish; and at times a band of youths fortified with strong waters, have stood watch there at that time, and have pretended to see strange sights, but their accounts thereof have differed and have not withstood examination. So that I held it my duty just before the Yuletide of last year to give a discourse on the Witch of Endor, taking occasion to rebuke those who would profess to acquaintance with familiar spirits.

Nevertheless, some of the godless, and I fear there are many such here, notwithstanding my labours, did make bold to visit the said churchyard. The results, as herein chronicled, were communicated to me by Zachary Hantorne, one of the aforementioned watchers, who contracted such a chill upon that occasion, that he shortly after departed from this life of mortal breath. Shortly before his decease, having certain soul stirrings, he sent for me in all haste, in order to unburden his sinful mind. The remainder of the story, concerning the part played by the illdoers of Moulton, was afterwards told to me by David Selby, an ungodlie man, alas of this parish, who betrayed the determined visit of the unrighteous of this village to Buckton Greene, unto certain dwellers in the parish of Moulton. The events described in their stories I have herewith set out in order.

Shortly before last Yuletide there was gathered together one dark and stormy night at the hostelry of Ye White Harte a profane and unhallowed company, ye chief of whom was Jonas White, a weaver of this parish of Kyngsthorpe. The subject of their unrighteous discourse was concerning ye strange apparition said to appear on the eve of Yuletide amidst the graves of Buckton Churchyard. The more sober of the party essayed to moderate the heat of the arguments, but Jonas White, being full of the potent liquor, continually asserted he was afraid of neither mortal nor ghost. Upon this, Robert Bletsoe offered to wager his three years old steer against the two pigs of Jonas White, that the weaver dared not upon the eve of Yuletide at the hour of midnight wend his way through the churchyard of the aforementioned Buckton Green. The drunken weaver not only accepted the wager, but, being puffed up with conceit of himself, affirmed that he would also take a hank of yarn from his store, and wind it in and out amongst the graves of the churchyard. The wager being witnessed by all the company, it was determined that on Yuletide eve this ungodlie gathering should again assemble at Ye White Harte to start thence at ten of the clock for Buckton Greene. In the interim, David Selby determined to play a mighty prank upon this assembly, and to cause them a great fright. For this purpose he made a journey to some of his kinsfolk dwelling in the parish of Moulton, and there related to them all this, which had been determined upon. Presently a plot was fixed amongst them whereby a ghost habited in black should be caused to appear in the churchyard at the hour of twelve on the night of the meeting.

In the meantime, Robert Bletsoe, a greedy and covetous man, had been casting longing eyes upon the two fat pigs of Jonas White, and had already determined that they should become his property. He, knowing that the weaver, when fortified with strong liquor, would dare to do that which he had wagered, made secret resolve with himself to scare the boaster from doing his intention by presenting himself as a ghost clothed in white, whereby he hoped that the weaver would be so mortally afraid as to flee, when this ghostly being should show itself. By means of this subtle strategy he hoped to obtain the pigs.

Accordingly, upon the eve of Yuletide, there was gathered together in the hostelry of Ye White Harte aforementioned, an impious band of miscreants bent upon doing sacrilege in the hallowed ground of our Lord and Saviour, adjoining Buckton Green.

Some great length of time was spent in mirth and revelry, and in the imbibing of strong liquor, whereby the company hoped to fortify their weak and carnal bodies against the fearful sightes which they looked forward to happen.

Presently, at ten of the clock, Robert Bletsoe pressed the assembly to make a start upon their way. So that for some time there was a great ado by reason of the lighting of lanterns, and the groping for thick oaken cudgels wherewith the watchers were arming themselves. Thus prepared, the crowd set out for their trystying place by way of the road to Moulton, which adjoins the Royal Park. After sundry waiting upon the road caused by the extinguishing of divers lanterns, and by the immersion of William Fasan in a mud hole by the road, ye motley company arrived at the churchyard at just past eleven of the clock. The moon was high in the heavens, lighting up the graves to all. Still keeping close as a flock of sheep, they disposed themselves to wait the hour of midnight.

In the meantime the ungodlie of Moulton had been searching near and far for some one to dress as a ghost, according to the plan. No person could be found willing to undertake this unholy duty until at length it was reported that in ye Blue Bell there lay a highwayman, who had drunken excess of strong waters. Him they took and gave more liquor until at length he had no concernment of that which was going on around. Then they stripped the poor wretch of his clothes, and smeared his body with honey, and afterwards covered the sticky mess with soot, so that he looked more like a poor black heathen man than like a true borne Englishman.

The poor drunken was then conveyed to the small wood on the

north side of the churchyard, there to await the hour of midnight.

At length the bells of Moulton rang out the midnight of Our Lord His birthday. Jonas White, with an ashen face and trembling knees, prepared to fulfil that which he had wagered, and started with his skein of thread down the path. At the same moment the men of Moulton waked the drunken highwayman, and forced him up the other end of the pathway. Robert Bletsoe, who had left the company from Kyngsthorpe, like a thief in the night, now appeared, attired all in white, at the eastern side of the churchyard. The three met in the middle. Jonas White, overwrought by terror, fell upon the ground behind a gravestone, his face to the earth, moaning and muttering, and beseeching the Lord to help him out of his pitiable plight.

Robert Bletsoe, on seeing the figure in black, thought it must be the ghost of the notorious Captain Slash, a highwayman, who formerly carried on his ungodlie calling in this and neighbouring parishes. Instantly he fled, his arms waving and uttering fearful cries at the same time, towards the place where the men of Moulton were hidden. They supposing him to be a ghost indeed fled for their lives back to their homes, where in whispers they told of the strange and supernatural signs they had seen. The drunken highwayman, who was too much overcome with liquor to have room for fear in his body, continued his march up the path, at the top of which were the watchers of Kyngsthorpe. They seeing a figure all in black, took him to be the very fiend himself, and fled, nor cast a look behind.

The highwayman was found next morning by the road to Moulton, sleeping off the effects of his drunken orgy.

Robert Bletsoe made his way home by a devious way, and Jonas White, after waiting for the dawn before venturing to move, rose to his feet and returned a chastened man.

Since that time both have come to me to determine which won the wager, but being a servant of the Lord, I gave them a discourse upon the sin of gambling and declared the pigs and steer forfeit to the church for a thank offering for their deliverance on that eventful night, which same should pay the cost of repairs to the western doorway.

Having laid the ghosts my story is finished, so I may now say with immortal William Shakespeare, sometime of Stratford-on-the-Avon, 'Alls well that ends well.'

Northamptonshire Notes and Queries, *Vol III, p 309-310.*

Trials, Examination and Condemnation

Witchcraft was rife throughout the county in the seventeenth and eighteenth centuries and Northamptonshire was the scene of many deeds of witchcraft and subsequent executions. Elinor Shaw of Cotterstock and Mary Phillips of Oundle pawned their souls to the devil in exchange for evil powers. When eventually found guilty they were condemned to a horrible death. Their execution was the last in the county and possibly the country.

At Northampton Assizes, on Wednesday the 7th of March 1705 for Bewitching a Woman, and two children, Tormenting them in a sad and lamentable manner till they Dyed.

With an Account of their strange Confessions, about their Familiarity with the Devil, and how they made a wicked Contract with him, to be revenged on several Persons, Bewitching their Cattel to Death, &c. and several other strange and amazing Particulars.

On Wednesday the 7th of this Instant March 1705, being the second day of the Assizes held at Northampton: One Elinor Shaw, and Mary Phillips, (two notorious Witches) were brought into Court, and there Arraign'd at the Bar, upon several Indictments of Witchcraft; particularly for Bewitching and Tormenting in a Diabolical manner, the Wife of Robert Wise of Benefield, in the said County till she Dyed, as also for Killing by Witchcraft, and wicked Facination, one Elizabeth Gorham of Glapthorn, a Child of about four Years of Age in the said County of Northampton; as also for Bewitching to Death, one Charles Ireland of Southwick in the said County; to which indictment the two said Prisoners pleaded not Guilty, and thereupon put themselves upon their Tryals as followeth.

The first Evidence against them, was one Widdow Peak, who deposed, that she with two other Women, undertook to watch the said Prisoners after they had been Apprehended and that about Midnight, there appeared in the Room a little white Thing, about the bigness of a cat, which sat upon Mary Phillip's Lap, at which time she heard her, the said Mary Phillips say, then pointing to Elinor Shaw, that she was the Witch that Kill'd Mrs. Wise, by Roasting her Effiges in Wax, sticking it full of Pinns, and till it was all wasted, and all this she affirm'd was done the same Night Mrs. Wise Dyed in a sad and languishing Condition. Mrs Evans, deposed, that when Mrs. Wise first was taken ill, that she saw Elinor Shaw look out at the window, (it being opposite to her House) at which time, she heard her say, I have done her Business now I am sure; this Night I'll send the old Devil a New Years Gift, (next day being New Years Day) and well knowing this Elinor Shaw to be a reputed Witch, was so much concern'd at her Words, that she went then to see how Mrs Wise did, where she found her Tormented with such Pains, as exceeding those of a Women in Travel, which encreased to such a terrible Degree, that she Expired about 12 of the Clock, to the great amazment of all her Neighbours.

Another Evidence made Oath, that Elinor Shaw and Mary Phillips, being one Day at her House, they told her she was a Fool to live so Miserable as she did, and therefore if she was willing, they would send something that Night that would Relieve her, and being an ignorant Woman she consented, and accordingly the same Night, two little black Things, almost like Moles came into her Bed and sucked her lower Parts, repeating the same for two or three Nights after, till she was almost frighted out of her Sences, insomuch that she was forced to send for Mr. Danks, the Minister to Pray by her several Nights, before the said Imps would leave her: She also added that she heard the said Prisoners say, that they would be Revenged on Mrs. Wise, because she would not give them some Buttermilk.

Mrs. Todd of Southwick, deposed that Charles Ireland, being a Boy of about 12 years of Age, was taken with strange Fitts about Christmas last, continuing so by Intervals till twelf Day last, at which time he Barked like a Dogg, and when he was Recovered and come to himself, he would Distinctly describe Elinor Shaw and Mary Phillips, affirming them two to be the Authors of his Misfortune, tho he never saw them in his Life; so that Mrs Ireland the Boy's Mother, was advised to Cork up some of his Water in a stone Bottle, fill'd full of Pins and Needles, and to Bury it under the Fire Hearth, which being done accordingly, the two said Witches could not be quiet, till they came to the said House, and desired to have the said bottle taken up, which was not granted, till they had confessed the Matter, and promised never to do so again, but for all this the next Night but one, the said Boy was so violently Handled, that he Dyed in two hours time; and this Womans Testimoney was confirm'd by five or six other

Evidence at the same time.

The said Witches were Try'd a third time for Bewitching to Death Elizabeth Gorham of Glapthorn, on the 10 of February last, as also for Killing several Horses, Hogs and sheep, being the Goods of Matthew Gorham Father of the said Child aforesaid. The evidence against them to prove all this; was William Boss, and John Southwel; who deposed that being Constables of the said Town, they were Charged with the said Prisoners in their Custody, who threatning them with Death, if they did not Confess and promising them to let them go if they would Confess; after some little Whineing and Hanging about one anothers Necks, they both made this Confession.

"That living in one House together they contracted with the Devil about a Year ago, to sell their Souls to him, upon condition, he would enable them to do what Mischief they desired, against whom they pleased, either in Body, Goods or Children; upon which the same Night, they had each of them three Imps sent them as they were going to Bed, and at the same instant the Devil appeared to them in the shape of a tall black Man, and told them, that these Imps would always be at their Service, either to kill Man, Woman, Child, Hog, Cow, Sheep, or any other Creature, when they pleased to command them provided they let 'em Suck their Flesh every Night which being agree'd to, the Devil came to Bed to them both, and had Carnal Knowledge of 'em, as if a Man, only with this difference instead of being Warm, his Embraces was very Cold and unpleasant. And that the next Morning they sent four of their Imps to Kill two Horses of one John Webb of the said Town of Glapthorn, because he openly said there were Witches, and accordingly the Horses were found Dead in a Pond the same day; and two days after this they Kill'd four great Hoggs after the same manner belonging to Matthew Gorham, because he said they both look'd like Witches, and not thinking this Revenge sufficient the next day after they sent two imps a piece to destroy his Child being a little Girl of about four Years of Age, which was done accordingly in $2\frac{1}{2}$ Hours time notwithstanding all the Skill and Endeavour of able doctors to preserve it. They further confessed that; if the said Imps were not constantly imploy'd to do Mischief they had not their Healths, but when they were imploy'd they were very Healthful and Well. They further added, that the said Imps did often tell them in the night-time, in a hollow whispering low Voice which they plainly understood, that they should never feel Hell Tormets, and that they had Kill'd a Horse and two Cows of one Widdow Broughton because she deny'd them some Peascods last year, for which they had also struck her Daughter with Lameness, which would never be cured as long as either of them liv'd and accordingly she has continued so ever since."

The abovesaid Evidence further deposed that having thus extorted the said Confession from the Prisoners, they persuded them to set their hands to it, which was done accordingly, tho with very much difficulty, upon which the said Confession was produced in Court, and the Witness's to it Examin'd, who all deposed upon oath, that the said Confessions was made in their Hearing, and that they saw the said reputed Witches set their Marks to it, in the presence of ten witnesses.

Upon which the said Prisoners, were desired by the Court to declare, whether they own'd the said confession and the Marks thereunto Affixed or not, to which they both answered in the Negative, and thereupon made such a howling, and lamentable noise as never was heard before, to the amazement of the whole court, and deny'd every particular that was laid to their Charge; but the Court having heard the matter of Fact so positively asserted against them by several Evidences, and above all by their own Confessions, that after having given a Larned Charge to the Jury relating to ever particular Circumstance, they brought them in both Guilty of willful Murther and witchcraft, and accordingly the next day the Court was pleased to pronounce sentence of Death upon them, that is to say, To be Hang'd till they are almost Dead, and then surrounded with Faggots, Pitch, and other Combustable matter, which being set on Fire, their Bodies are to be consumed to Ashes.

As soon as they are Executed I will send you an Account of their Behaviour and last Dying Speeches.

March 8 1705

Yours Ralph Davis

Witchcraft In Northamptonshire, *1867*.

Concern amongst the Gentry

1ST FEBRUARY 1673

After hearing so much about witches, Holland asked Father for permission to go to Bowden to see everything for himself; Father agreed. So he went off very early in the morning and told us the whole story on his return. The father of these children, who have had charms and spells cast on them, is a weaver, who they say is a hard worker who has made quite a bit of money by his trade. He once went to Harborough to buy cheese, butter and other provisions. Meanwhile his wife, who stayed at home, decided to send the children to help their father home with his purchases; and before they left a woman came and said she would like to go to Harborough with them. But their mother was unwilling, since she had heard stories about the woman - there was a rumour that a man now on his deathbed had accused her of causing his death. Eventually, however, she consented. On the way the eldest girl said they had met a man who nodded to them. The woman said to him, 'Are you nodding at me, you impudent rogue? I'll send cats to haunt you.' This made the girl shudder, and not long afterwards she was bewitched and so were all the other children soon afterwards. When Branson related this to Father, he ordered them to examine the pillows; when they did this they found feathers stuck together in a remarkable way, with their ends coalescing; they threw them all on to the fire and burned them. Mrs Brown is one of those suspected of witchcraft; her husband was at the inn at about that time, and when asked how his wife was he said she was well but had already gone to bed. The boys and girls who were bewitched barked and mewed like dogs and cats and had the women's names constantly on their lips. But when the paroxysm was over they accused no one, saying that they were quite well and felt no pain. A woman who lived next door to one of the witches said that her door often creaked in the night and rendered sleep impossible. One of the women is put in prison and her children left to the parish for support.

The Diary of Thomas Isham of Lamport, *translated by N. Marlow, originally written 1671-73.*

14 · FOLKLORE, MYTHS AND LEGENDS

Air Ada

In the early twentieth century Reg Norman was the acknowledged expert of the dialect of central Northamptonshire. In the 1950's together with Peter Nevitt they produced a long newspaper series of cartoons featuring two characters; Air Ada (the name of the series) and Mawwud. Air Ada who always did the talking and Mawwud her silent partner. The following conversation is in the 'Air Ada' style.

CHEWIN' THE RAG!

Gert.   If it ent air Doris, 'ow are yer me duck?

Doris.   Well, gel, it aint arf luvly to see yer. Aryer cum dain tain to do yer Chrissmus shoppin'?

Gert.   No gel, my Arfur's gotta rite belly ake an' 'ackin corf an I gotta get sum corf mixcher an' sumthin' byndin in the way o' fizzick.

Doris.   Are bet yer feddup then, cos we all know wot men are like wen there porlee.

Gert.   Yis and the bab's got croop sos I kent stop ait menny minits gel, ain' I gotta goo an' get sum trotters for weir tea.

Doris.   Arm jus' gooing ter me cleanin' job, sis. Mrs 'arris is gotta a saw 'ead an' a sharp tung if arm late. Its mee day fer cleanin' them perishin' winders, an' in this brass monkey weather an' all, I arsk yer, 'ood be a char thees days? Thank Gawd we dunt 'ave ter scrub the frunt steps or black the grates no more, or do the dollying. We still atter polish the brassiz an' cleen up 'is dratted fag ash. Well, no good standin' ere chopsin' gel, I ent dun me carrots yit to goo wimmee ship's 'ead. Even me bikes gotta puncher an' air Bert's too idle to fix it, sittin' there on 'is be'ind in the back kitchun in 'is cap 'n scarf like Lord Muck, with 'is Woodie stuck in 'is face, with 'is jug o'stout, and air Cyral at the footer an' all.

Gert.　Men per! Who'd 'ave 'em? No good as use nor ornament, I alluz sez.

Doris.　Tadar air Gert, shladder be gooin, keep yer pecker up.

Gert.　Same to you me duck, 'appy bloomin' Chrissmus, 'ope yer got yer winter draws on, there's gonna be a sharp frorst ternight, ser long.

CHEWING THE RAG!

Gert.　If it isn't our Doris, how are you?

Doris.　Well, girl, it is lovely to see you. Have you come to town to do your Christmas shopping?

Gert.　No girl, my Arthur has got awful stomach ache and a hacking cough and I have to get some cough mixture and something binding in the way of medicine.

Doris.　I bet you are fed up then, because we all know what men are when they are poorly.

Gert.　Yes, and the baby's got whooping cough, so I can't stay out many minutes girl, and I must go and get some pig's feet for our tea.

Doris.　I'm just going to my cleaning job, sister. Mrs Harris has a sore head and a sharp tongue if I'm late. It's my day for cleaning those perishing windows and in this cold weather too. I ask you, who would be a charlady these days? Thank God, we don't have to scrub the front steps or black the grates, or do the dollying any more. We still have to polish the brasses and clean up his cigarette ash. Well, it's no good standing here gossiping, girl, I've not prepared my carrots yet to go with my sheep's head. Even my bicycle has a puncture and our Bert is too idle to fix it, sitting there on his backside in his cap and scarf, like Lord Muck, with his Woodbine stuck in his mouth, and his jug of stout, and Cyril is at the football match.

Gert.　Men, pooh, who would have them? No good as use or ornament, I always say.

Doris.　Cheerio, our Gert, keep your spirits up.

Gert.　Same to you. Happy Christmas. Hope you have got your winter drawers on, because there is going to be a sharp frost tonight! So long.

Mia Butler and Colin Eaton, Learn Yersalf Northamptonshire Dialect *(1998), pp 37-40.*

Proverbs and Sayings

Amusing sayings, many specific to an area, village or town.

More spires, more haughtiness, and less hospitality than any other county in England.

Northamptonshire, full of love
Benethe the gyrdyll and noth above.
Taken from 'Characteristics of the Counties' *by an anonymous Shropshire poet.*

Doddington dovecote,
Wilby hen,
Irthlingborough ploughboys,
And Wellingborough men.

If there's ice in November that will bear a duck.
The rest of the winter will be slush and muck.
If it rains on Easter Day.
Much good grass, but little good hay.

The mayor of Northampton opens Oysters with his dagger.
To keep them at a sufficient distance from his nose.
(Originated from Northampton being 80 miles from the sea, thus all fish were unlikely to be fresh.)

Thack and dyke
Northamptonshire like.
(Thack = thatch)

He that must eat a buttered faggot let him go to Northampton.
(Originated from Northamptonshire being the dearest town in England for fuel. This was before coal barges navigated the River Nene.)

Brackley Breed
Better to hang than to feed.
(Brackley was a decaying market town, troubling the country with its beggars.)

If a hare is seen in the village, a disaster such as a fire will occur within a month.

Harvest Home

It is customary to decorate the last or 'harvest load' with boughs of oak and ash, and the men, who all ride home upon it, sing with great gusto variations on the rhyme.

Harvest Home! Harvest Home!
Harvest Home!
We've plough'd,
We've sown,
We've ripp'd,
We've mown.
Harvest home! Harvest home!
We want water, and kaint get nun.

. . . in some areas of the county church bells are rung and the rhyme alters to,

Harvest home! Harvest home!
The boughs they do shake, and the bells they do ring;
So merrily we bring harvest in, harvest in;
So merrily we bring harvest in.

All these celebrations are often followed by the harvest suppers.

Two men come in covered with blankets stuffed with straw on their back, they call out as they come in, 'corks and blue,' and then sit down and call for ale, the scene being a public house. They begin to drink and run over droll stories and recollections of their former travels, etc. One, seeming more covetous of beer than the other (whose tongue keeps him employed), takes, every now and then, a pull at the tankard, as opportunity offers, unknown to his talkative companion, in consequence of which the tankard is often empty and filled; and on calling for the reckoning, the other, who has been busied in discourse, starts, surprised at the largeness of the bill and refuse payment. The other, nearly drunk, reels and staggers about, and stubbornly resists all persuasions of satisfaction on his part, which brings on a duel with their long staves, driving each other out of the room as a termination to the scene.

The Dialect and Folk-Lore of Northamptonshire, *T. Sternberg, 1851, p 176-178.*

A Northamptonshire Jingle

Abington, Addington, Boddington, Doddington,
  Bainton, Barton, Hinton, Horton,
Elmington, Elkington, Luddington, Loddington,
  Slipton, Slapton, Knuston, Norton.

Hannington, Harrington, Overstone, Oxendon,
  Gayton, Glendon, Glinton, Weston,
Warmington, Werrington, Hackleton, Piddington,
  Moulton, Milton, Easton Neston.

Geddington, Harrowden, Hellidon, Hardingstone,
  Brington, Brampton, Braunston, Charlton,
Middleton, Nassington, Duddington, Farthingstone,
  Weldon, Weedon, Welton, Carlton.

Ailsworth, Arthingworth, Harringworth, Blisworth,
  Astcote, Duncote, Eastcote, Burcote,
Culworth, Greatworth, Theddingworth, Brixworth,
  Holcot, Hulcot, Huscote, Murcote.

Barford, Dodford, Cranford, Denford,
  Blakesley, Brackley, Catesby, Mawsley,
Heyford, Lilford, Maidford, Thenford,
  Daventry, Pytchley, Naseby, Fawsley.

Irthlingborough, Sudborough, Litchborough, Peterborough,
  Cogenhoe, Farthinghoe, Furtho, Wadenhoe,
Silverstone, Haselbech, Pattishall, Wellingborough,
  Rockingham, Wappenham, Passenham, Stowe.

Kislingbury, Lamport, Kingsthorpe, Middlethorpe,
  Brafield, Byfield, Hollowell, Lowick,
Newbottle, Nobottle, Blatherwycke, Thorpe,
  Maidwell, Pipewell, Scaldwell, Crick.

The Northampton County Magazine, *1928, p 20*.

Northamptonshire's Pancake Jingle

The pancake bell was originally rung on Shrove Tuesday, calling people to church where the priest would be ready to listen to their confessions.

Pancakes and fritters,
Says the bells of St Peter's.
Where must we fry 'em?
Says the bells of Cold Higham.
In yonder land thurrow,
Says the bells of Wellingborough.
You owe me a shilling,
Says the bells of Great Billing.
When will you pay me?
Says the bells at Middleton Cheney.
When I am able,
Says the bells at Dunstable.
That will never be,
Says the bells at Coventry.
Oh yes, it will,
Says Northampton Great Bell.
White bread and sop,
Says the bells at Kingsthrop.
Trundle a lantern,
Says the bells at Northampton.

(thurrow = furrow)

The bells of the churches of Northampton were also rung and the following was said as a similar doggerel:

Roast beef and marsh mallows,
Say the bells of All Hallow's.
Pancakes and fritters,
Says the bells of St. Peter's.
Roast beef and boil'd,
Says the bells of St. Giles.
Pokers and tongs,

> Says the bells of St. Johns,
> Shovell, tongs and poker,
> Says the bells of St. Pulchre's

St. Pulchre's = Holy Sepulchre Church

Northamptonshire Words and Phrases, Baker, 1854, Vol II, p 91, 92.

Superstitions

Amusing local superstitions are interesting to read, but in many cases no longer recognised or maybe even forgotton.

If a female is afflicted with fits, nine pieces of silver money and nine three half-pences are collected from nine bachelors; the silver money is converted into a ring to be worn by the afflicted person, and the money (ie. 13fid) is paid to the maker of the ring, an inadequate remuneration for his labour, but which he good-naturedly accepts. If the afflicted person be a male the contributions are levied upon females.

At the beginning of the century in the villages of north-west Northamptonshire, fried mice were given as a specific for whooping-cough. The children were decoyed by nurses into eating them by being told they were small birds.

Sale by 'Pin and Candle'

A curious and ancient custom has just been observed at the village of Corby, near Kettering, where the land belonging to the parish charities has been let by the interesting old custom of a burning candle. A pin was inserted in the candle a short distance from the light, and the bidding advanced until the pin dropped. The ceremony was directed by the rector (Rev B.E.W. Bennett) and was attended by many parishioners. Bidding was brisk, and the fall of the pin was watched with considerable interest. When the heat dislodged the pin the last bidder found that they had the land on a lease of eight years.

A crow alighting at a short distance in front of a person going along a road is looked upon as the forerunner of bad luck; two crows alighting in the same way are said to be a sign of good luck, particularly if, when flying away, the crows go over the person's head; while four crows prognosticate a death in the person's family. A single white pigeon is considered a bird of evil omen; if, after hovering around for some time, it finally alights upon a house, it is said to be a warning of the approaching death of one of the inmates of the house.

Northamptonshire Notes and Queries, *Vol 1-6, 1886-92.*

And Something for the Inner Man

Traditional food, some associated with a feast or celebration, others generally of the county. Try this . . .

BOILED BEEF AND CARROTS

This meal must be made with cooked beef so if all you have is raw meat then cut it into bite sized pieces and place it in boiling water for long enough to thoroughly seal it. The advantage of using cooked meat is that the gravy remains clear; clear gravy and lots of it is the secret of this meal. When everything else has been eaten it can be mopped up with a couple of slices of good thick bread.

INGREDIENTS

To make the casserole: 12 oz (340g) cooked beef, 6 oz (170g) carrots, 2 medium leeks, 4 oz (115g) turnips, parsnips and/or swede as available. A stick of celery is optional.

To make the dumplings: 2 oz (55g) self raising flour, 1 oz (30g) shredded suet, a pinch of salt, water.

METHOD

Cut the beef into bite sized pieces and place in a casserole. Peel and slice the carrots, cut the celery stick into approximately fi inch (1cm) lengths and dice the remaining vegetables, putting them all in the casserole. Place the casserole in an oven at 250°F/120°C (Gas Mark fi) for two hours. While it is cooking place the flour, suet and salt in a mixing bowl and mix in a little water very gradually until it has the consistency of dough. Break the dough into four equal sized pieces and roll into balls on a floured board. After the casserole has been cooking for about one and a half hours add the dumplings and cook for a further one and a half hours. Serve this dish with boiled potatoes and a couple of slices of dry bread per person.

Traditional Northamptonshire Recipes, *I. Andrews, 2000, W.D. Wharton, p 150.*

LIST OF SOURCES

Textual sources are listed below alphabetically by author's name and indicate the title and the date of the edition consulted, although this is not necessarily the earliest version and in some cases editions were not dated. In the main text the date given with the author's name is either the date of the first publication or, when appropriate, the dates of the author's birth and death.

In some cases I have abridged or sub-edited in order that an extract settles comfortably in its new surroundings and gives an interesting reading.

Addis, Ian: *Moments of the Rose*. Jema Publications 1994

Andrews, Ian: *Traditional Northamptonshire Recipes*. W.D.Wharton 2001

Bell, Thomas: *The Rural Album*, 1853

Blagrove, David: *Braunston ... a Canal History*, 1995

Brown, Mike and Willmott, Brian: *Brewed in Northants*. A Brewery History Society Publication 1998

Butler, M & Eaton, C: *Learn Yersalf Northamptonshire Dialect*. Nostalgic Press

Cole G.D.H. & Browning D.C: *Daniel Defoe, A Tour Through the Whole Island of Great Britain*. Everyman 1962

Cushing, K: *A History of the Hospital of St John's Northampton*.

Davies, Nicholas: *The Princess Who Changed The World*. Blake Publishing 1997

Deacon, Malcolm: *Philip Doddridge of Northampton 1702-1751*. Northamptonshire Libraries 1980

Dickens, Charles: *Bleak House*. Oxford University Press 1991

Dickens, Charles: *The Posthumous Papers of The Pickwick Club*

Drayton, Michael: *Poly-olbion*, 1622

Fell, Bryan: *The Houses of Parliament An Illustrated Guide*. Eyre & Spottiswoods, 1965

Flower, Raymond: *Oundle and the English Public School*. Stacey International 1989

Freeling, A: *The London and Birmingham Railway Companion*, 1838

Fuller, Thomas: *History of the Worthies of England*, 1662

Gordon, Peter: *Politics and Society, The Journals of Lady Knightley of Fawsley 1885 to 1913*. Northamptonshire Record Society 1999

Gordon, Peter: *The Wakes of Northamptonshire*. Northamptonshire Libraries 1992

Grimes, Dorothy: *Like Dew Before The Sun* 1991

Harrison, M: *The Centenary History of St Matthew's Church and Parish in Northampton.* Pentland Press 1993

Hassell, John: *A Tour of the Grand Junction Canal in 1819.* Cranfield and Bonfiel Books 1968

Headway House Education Group: *Commemoration of Manfield,* 1992

Hold, Trevor: *A Northamptonshire Garland.* Northamptonshire Libraries 1989

Jenkins, Eric: *Northamptonshire Murder Tales.* Cordelia 1998

Jenkins, Eric: *Victorian Northamptonshire Scandals and Surprises of 1840-1841.* W.D. Wharton 1999

Marlow, N: The Diary of Thomas Isham of Lamport 1671-73. Gregg International 1971

Marshall, F: *Witchcraft In Northamptonshire.* J Taylor and Son 1866

Mee, Arthur: *The King's England, Northamptonshire.* Hodder and Stoughton Ltd 1949

Northampton Borough Council: *Northampton Remembers The Guildhall.* N.B.C. 1989

Northampton Borough Council: *Northampton Remembers Boot and Shoe.* N.B.C. 1988

Northamptonshire County Magazine Volume I 1928, Volume IV 1931, Volume 5 1932, Volume 6 1933

Northamptonshire Federation of Women's Institutes: *Northamptonshire Within Living Memory.* Countryside Books 1992

Northamptonshire Notes and Queries Volume I to VI 1854 to 1894

Northamptonshire Past and Present 1956, 1957, 1960, 1961, 1966/67

Parker, David: *Oundle in the News.* Spiegl Press 1998

Pierce, Edward: *A Contemporary Account of the Fire of Northampton 1675.* Northamptonshire Libraries 1974

Pipe, Marian: *Ghosts and Folklore of Northamptonshire* Vol III. Spiegl Press 1986

Rogers, Byron: *An Audience With An Elephant.* Aurum Press 2001

Salmon, J: *English Teatime Recipes.* J Salmon Press

Savage, Anne: *The Anglo Saxon Chronicles.* Salamander Books 2002

Slater, Don: *Sywell The Parish and the People.* Jema Publications 2002

Spelman, J: *Voices of the Nene Valley.* Tempus Publishing 2001

Steane, J.M: *The Northamptonshire Landscape.* Hodder and Stoughton Ltd 1974

Sternberg, Thomas: *The Dialect and Folk-Lore of Northamptonshire.* S. R. Publishers 1971

Woodall, David: *The Mobbs Own.* Northamptonshire Regiment Association 2000

Worledge, J. & V: *The Northamptonshire Poetry and Sketches of George Harrison* (1876-1950). Jema Publications 1996

ACKNOWLEDGEMENTS

I am grateful to the following for allowing the inclusion of both prose and poetry which remains in copyright; Hodder and Stoughton Limited for J. M. Stean's *Northamptonshire Landscape*; Northamptonshire Libraries for 'In Praise of Northamptonshire' by Trevor Hold; *The Spectator* for 'England's Best Market Square' by John Betjeman; Northampton Record Society for several pieces from *Politics and Society, The Journals of Lady Knightley of Fawsley 1885-1913* by Prof. Peter Gordon; the Chrysalis Group for extracts from The *Anglo Saxon Chronicles* translated by Anne Savage; W.D. Wharton for extracts from *Traditional Northamptonshire Recipes* by Ian Andrews; several extracts from *The Diary of Thomas Isham of Lamport 1671-73* translated by N. Marlow; Northamptonshire Libraries and Information Service for the article 'The road will last a thousand years' taken from *The Wakes of Northamptonshire* by Prof. Peter Gordon, and Sir Hereward Wake, Bart., M.C.; for the extract from *The Centenary History of St Matthew's Church and Parish* by M. Harrison; Cordelia and Eric Jenkins for the article in *Northamptonshire Murder Tales*; Northamptonshire Regiment Association for the extract from *The Mobbs Own*; Countryside Books for the items from the Northamptonshire Federation of Women's Institutes *Northamptonshire Within Living Memory*; Stacey International for the article from *Oundle and the English Public School* by Raymond Flower; Tempus Books for the item in *Voices of the Nene Valley*; Spiegl Press for the item from *Ghosts and Folklore of Northamptonshire*; Aurum Press for the item from *An Audience with an Elephant*; Headway House Educational Group for *The Grey Lady*; items from *Learn Yersalf Northamptonshire Dialect*; J. Salmon Ltd, Sevenoaks, England for Northamptonshire Seed Cake in *English Teatime Recipes*; Arthur Mee's *Northamptonshire* (The King's England series is reprinted by The King's England Press, who kindly allowed the inclusion of the extract). Also thanks to Jema Publications and the authors who have allowed me to reprint their items.

The Northamptonshire engravings that decorate the chapter headings are taken from *Northamptonshire Poetry and Sketches of George Harrison 1876 to 1950* by John and Vera Worledge, *Wanderers In Northamptonshire* Volume 1 and 2 by John and Vera Worledge, and *Northamptonshire Past and Present*, Volume II, No 6.

Special thanks are due to Alison Cowling, the Keeper of the Fine Arts at Northampton Museum, and to Northampton Museums and Art Gallery, for allowing the use of *The Cock Inn, Kingsthorpe* by Albert E. Bailey on the front cover.